100 Easy-to-Grow
Native Plants

On a sunny slope in a northwestern garden, species such as the pink Hooker's onion (*Allium acuminatum*), horsetail (*Equisetum arvense*), and the white-flowered Labrador tea (*Ledum groenlandicum*) flourish.

100

EASY-TO-GROW

NATIVE
PLANTS

FOR CANADIAN GARDENS

UPDATED

LORRAINE JOHNSON

PHOTOGRAPHS
BY ANDREW LEYERLE

whitecap

A DENISE SCHON BOOK

Updated edition copyright © 2005
Denise Schon Books Inc.
Originally published in 1999
Text copyright © 1999 Lorraine Johnson
Photographs copyright © 1999 Andrew Leyerle

Whitecap Books
Vancouver/Toronto
www.whitecap.ca

A DENISE SCHON BOOK

Library and Archives Canada Cataloguing in Publication

Johnson, Lorraine, 1960–
    100 easy-to-grow native plants for Canadian gardens / Lorraine
Johnson ; photographs by Andrew Leyerle. – 2nd ed.

ISBN 1-55285-657-7

    1. Native plant gardening – Canada. I. Title. II. Title: One
hundred easy-to-grow native plants for Canadian gardens.

SB439.26.C3J629 2005   635.9'5171   C2004-907077-0

Produced by: Denise Schon Books Inc.
Design: Counterpunch/Linda Gustafson
Editorial: Wendy Thomas

Printed and bound in Canada by Friesens

10   9   8   7   6   5   4   3   2

*The author and photographer would like to thank
all those gardeners who so generously shared their
experiences and their gardens with us.*

*We thank the following institutions
for allowing access to their gardens:
Photographs on pp. 21, 55, 66, 78, 86, 104, 135
courtesy of Holden Arboretum, Ohio
Photographs on pp. 58, 71, 74, 97, 132
courtesy of Casa Loma, Toronto
Photographs on p. 129 courtesy of Chicago Botanic Garden*

OTHER BOOKS BY LORRAINE JOHNSON
The Gardener's Manifesto (paperback; *Tending the Earth*,
    hardcover)
The New Ontario Naturalized Garden
*Grow Wild! Native Plant Gardening in Canada and
    Northern United States*
Suggestive Poses: Artists and Critics Respond to Censorship
*The Real Dirt: The Complete Guide to Backyard, Balcony
    and Apartment Composting* (co-authored with Mark
    Cullen)
Green Future: How to Make a World of Difference

CONTENTS

FOREWORD TO THE NEW EDITION

In the years since the first edition of this book was published, interest in native plants has grown exponentially. When I give talks and slide shows, it seems that almost everyone in the audience has at least some native plants in their gardens. Cruising the aisles at nurseries, I notice that many now have sections devoted to native plants. And every year, the number of non-profit organizations that include native plant education as part of their mandate increases.

I think that the roots of this interest can be found in the yearning many of us feel for a better, more environmentally sane world. We might feel relatively powerless in the face of global environmental problems, but in the purview of our gardens – the tiny bits of land we steward – we can make a positive difference, creating small places of beauty and ecosystem health. While we no doubt need more powerful tools to effect change on a large scale (climate change and endangered species and spaces come to mind), I'm convinced that a simple trowel is a grand place to start the necessary (and, in moments of hope, I think inevitable) transformation of our culture from nature dominance to nature partnership. Dig in – the roots of change need to be anchored deep ...

Much of the species information in this edition remains the same as in the first edition, as does the section on propagation. The nursery listings have been changed and updated. There are a number of references in the introduction to my own backyard garden. I have not changed this text, but I have moved since I wrote this book. My new, relatively small, downtown garden (all lawn when we first moved in a couple of years ago) offers endless opportunities for experimentation – thirty new trees and counting, a small meadow that will get shadier with each year, eventually turning (returning, really) to woodland, a shrub garden out front for the birds, a fern and sedge garden for my partner, and a profound lesson in time and transformation for me ...

LIST OF ENTRIES

The author's low-maintenance meadow garden virtually looks after itself. The lounge chair, and not the weeding pad, was the most-used gardener's tool during the summer.

INTRODUCTION

Wary readers may wonder what exactly I mean by the title's phrase "easy-to-grow." Anyone who has been stung by another gardener's insistence that triple-trench-digging an acre and a half is "easy" will recognize that facility is a relative concept. So I'd like to put it in context.

My small backyard garden (16 by 10 feet/4.8 by 3 m) is a native plant meadow (though there are a few non-natives – for example, a lilac bush, a concession to my partner, which seems only fair, since I've monopolized the rest of the garden!). Recently, I was asked to be part of a study to assess the amount of time and inputs (water, fertilizers, etc.) various types of gardens require. In addition to my native plant meadow, the survey looked at a typical lawn and a conventional flower garden, among other landscape styles. For the whole growing season, I kept a logbook itemizing exactly how much time I spent working in my garden – that is, how much watering, fertilizing, weeding, mowing I did. I also kept track of exactly how much in the way of material inputs went in to the garden – the survey people asked me to measure water by the bucketful, chemicals by the ounce, gas for the mower by the gallon, expenses by the nickel, and so on.

I've always known that my garden was a low-maintenance project and that I spent far more time sitting on the patio than weeding on all fours, but when I tabulated the results of my season-long record-keeping, I was shocked to discover just how low maintenance it is. The grand total of time I spent on garden maintenance from the spring through to autumn: 3 hours and 15 minutes. Total. That includes weeding, watering, pruning, deadheading, digging, dividing, transplanting...everything. When I say "easy-to-grow," I mean it quite literally.

This is not to say that I couldn't have spent more time working in the garden had I chosen to. The lilac certainly would have benefited from being liberated from its native clematis vine (*Clematis virginiana*) shroud; by mid-summer, the vine had covered the shrub and I should have done some hacking. And had I done any weeding in early spring, I'm sure I could have trimmed back on my grand total of weeding time in mid-summer (45 minutes). And perhaps I should have watered the thirsty Joe-pye weed during the August drought. But other pleasures beckoned, and 3.25 hours of allround garden maintenance it was.

There have been no dire consequences from my season of sloth. The Joe-pye weed perked up after a good rain. Underneath a billowy cloud of clematis flowers and seedheads at the end of the season, the lilac leaves looked green, a sure sign of life. And all the spent blossoms of the ironweed and cup plant that I didn't bother deadheading went to seed and fed the birds. In other words, not only did nature facilitate my laziness, but nature also redeemed it with reward, too.

Perhaps this is one of the main lessons to be learned from the native plant garden. Nature is pretty much in control of things. Sure, the gardener can tinker away, as temperament and the need for soothing work-time in the garden demand, or the gardener can take low maintenance to the extreme outer reaches (as I seem to have done that summer), but at the end of the day the native plant garden continues . . . on its own steam.

Which explains my survey results in the "input" categories. Water? A total of 30 liters (about 8 gallons) directed exclusively at four seedlings I put in in the spring and needed to water until they got established. Other than that, the rain did my watering work – even during a very dry summer. Gas? No lawn, so no endless mowing and no fossil fuel or electrical energy use. Fertilizers? The meadow plants don't need any. (Indeed, I wouldn't want my 10 foot/3 m-tall cup plant and 8 foot/2.4 m-tall sunflower to get any healthier! They'd be giant genetic monsters if I fed them any fertilizers.)

Chemicals? Zilch. My garden is organic on principle and organic in practice, and through its life, I've yet to encounter a pest problem that couldn't be dealt with using soap and water. Most other native plant gardeners I've talked with across North America report the same thing. It's the adapt or die principle in action – native plants have evolved over thousands of years to the conditions found in their home range, so they don't succumb to pest attack with the same regularity as exotic plants. Anyone who doubts this should plant a native woodland

groundcover beside a hosta, which is non-native, and see which plant the slugs devour. The exotic hosta, guaranteed. Actually, my neighbor and I enact this experiment every summer. He pours on the slug poison and I pour on the native seeds, five feet (1.5 m) away. The slugs in my garden are more than happy to ignore my natives and instead spend their lives in the compost bin (where they're useful); my neighbor's slugs, on the other hand, are happily munching their way through a third expensive hosta planting. (My neighbor is now at the point where he hides the chemicals as I walk up the drive – I think he's starting to see that there's something, well, deeply humiliating about battling a slug.)

In case this is starting to sound like unseemly gardener-one-upmanship, I should note that my neighbor has a lovely garden, and that my meadow is not to everyone's taste. No single garden ever is. Anyone with claustrophobia would find my towering plants dizzying, and even in such a small plot, one could get lost in foliage on the trip to the compost bin. But the look of my garden is dictated by my particular choices of native plants, not the fact that I've chosen to garden with natives. If I wanted a more restrained style, I could easily choose from the dazzling array of natives with more compact growth. And that, essentially, is one of the beauties of native plant gardening: the incredible diversity from which to choose. Whatever your conditions – shady, sunny, or somewhere in between – and whatever your desired style – formal, informal, or a mix of the two – you can find many natives to suit your needs and achieve your goals.

The hundred easy-to-grow native plants detailed in this book (and the dozens of others referred to in various sections throughout) represent just a fraction of the native plants appropriate for the garden setting. It was next to impossible (and more than a little heartbreaking) to limit my choices to a hundred. I was guided, however, by the principle that, along with being easy to grow, all should be relatively easy to find in the nursery trade and most should be ones I'd actually grown. My own experiences in cultivating these plants have been supplemented by many fruitful exchanges with dozens of other native plant gardeners across North America who have so generously shared their adventures with me.

One final word about the hundred. Readers alert to mathematic precision will note that there are actually 101. Consider it the baker's dozen principle. Or the gardener's guilty pleasure principle: there's always room for one more.

I neglected to mention one personally significant finding of that survey. The money I spent on my garden all summer? Not a penny.

HOW TO USE THIS BOOK

Let's just admit it: gardeners tend to be voyeuristic creatures and plant lists are our chaste form of porn. There's little competition in the ecstasy department for the thrill of finding the perfect plant. (Move over Harlequin: aching desire applies equally to horticulture.) So I urge you to browse through this book with your yearn-radar set on high. Some of these plants have a simple, subtle beauty; others are brassy and more declarative; each will enhance the garden.

The plant listings are divided into a number of categories, and the following represents some general things to keep in mind while reading through and using the information in this book.

WHAT IS A NATIVE PLANT? A native plant is a plant that grew in a region prior to European settlement. Native plants have evolved over time in association with the many other plants and animals that also occur naturally in the region. Confusingly, not all "wildflowers" (meaning, simply, plants that grow in the wild, without human cultivation) are native plants; some, such as dandelions and Queen Anne's lace, arrived in North America with the European settlers. These human introductions are known as non-native plants, exotics, aliens, introduced species – or, sometimes, weeds. All of the plants discussed in this book are native to various regions of North America. To learn about the hundreds of other plants native to your region, consult a field guide.

COMMON NAME: There's often confusion surrounding common names, so be careful when buying plants to confirm that you've got the species you want – check the common name against the Latin name. For example, I've listed *Heliopsis helianthoides* by its common name false sunflower. However, it's also known as ox-eye, which gets confusing because there's a non-native plant called ox-eye daisy. There are numerous colloquial variations, so check the Latin.

BOTANICAL NAME: Every plant has a botanical Latin name (a binomial), which consists of two parts: the first part identifies the plant's genus and the second part, the plant's species name. Though many plants share the same genus, each species is separate and distinct.

In this book, I have not listed cultivars, named varieties, or hybrids – the results of the genetic tinkering plant breeders do to "improve" wild species. There's some measure of botanical nostalgia in my decision, but there's also an ecological imperative: I figure that 10,000 years of genetic history and adaptation, inherent in each plant's evolution, is worth honoring, depending on and deferring to, rather than messing with. Besides – and no offense to the plant breeders – the tinkerers are the same people who brought us the tasteless red package known as the commercial tomato. So I encourage you to seek out the native species form of these plants (identified simply by their Latin binomial, *Monarda didyma*, for example) rather than the named varieties, cultivars, or hybrids (which are easy to identify by the names added to the Latin – for example, *Monarda didyma* 'Cambridge Scarlet').

HEIGHT: For the most part, I have followed the height ranges listed in field guides such as Peterson's and Audubon's, unless personal experience dictates otherwise. In the garden setting, where plants are sometimes coddled, they may grow taller than in the wild.

BLOOMING PERIOD: There's so much variation, caused by a host of factors such as elevation, annual vagaries, etc., that a precise designation of a specific month for blooming is not possible. Use the periods given as a guideline, and expect that some years, the plant that usually blooms in late spring will last into mid-summer or that your perfect late-summer combination might grace the fall garden.

EXPOSURE: A useful – and obvious – guideline to follow is that woodland plants need shade and that meadow and prairie plants need sun. But this only takes us so far. Early-spring bloomers in the deciduous woodland garden actually thrive in quite a bit of sun before the tree canopy leafs out. And meadow plants that grow naturally on the forest edge can cope with a surprising amount of shade in the garden. If you're at all in doubt about whether your light conditions are appropriate for a specific plant, cross-reference the "Habitat" section of the listing too – "open woods," for example, will indicate a good degree of flexibility in terms of partial sun or partial shade. Don't be afraid to experiment. The term partial shade is somewhat vague – use it as a guideline. If you have a few hours of shade, that should be fine for most plants that require partial shade conditions. Open shade refers to the kind of light that occurs in woodlands with high canopy trees.

MOISTURE: All plants have a moisture preference (and, again, habitat is a clue), ranging from wet through moist and average to dry, but many plants will also do well in a broad range of conditions. I've listed each plant's natural moisture regime, but also noted when a plant's requirements are more flexible. With a few exceptions – easily identified as such in the listing – most plants in this book will do fine in the average garden's soil conditions.

HABITAT: In the wild, all plants grow in a particular kind of community or habitat. Convention allows for somewhat broad labels (woodland, meadow, prairie, wetland, for example), but within each of these habitat designations it is possible to get increasingly specific. The woodland, for example, may be a deciduous or evergreen forest; more specific still, it may be an oak woodland, a maple/beech woodland, or a coastal conifer forest.

The broad label of prairie habitat may also be broken down into various types: for example, tall-grass, mixed-grass, and shortgrass prairie, depending on location (tallgrass in the easternmost prairie region, shortgrass in the western). As well, please note that prairie is used in this category to refer to a habitat type; it is also used in the next section, "Range," to refer to a geographic range or location. One way to avoid confusion is to remember that within the geographically defined prairie region, there are different types of habitats ranging from prairie habitat to woodland, wetland, and meadow habitats. But when "prairie" is used to define habitat rather than range, it means just that: a prairie plant community of grasses and wildflowers.

The term meadow habitat is a rather slippery category; ecologists and botanists continue to debate what exactly it means. For the purposes of this book, I use the term to signify a plant community that is neither prairie nor woodland, but rather is a transitional community. (In the wild, meadow communities develop when a gap opens up in the forest; sun-loving species move in and thrive for many years, but slowly the meadow evolves into a forest again, as shade-loving woodland species take hold.) Many meadow plants are adapted to partially shady conditions as well as full sun, and many are ideal for urban gardens because they thrive in disturbed, nutrient-poor soil.

The habitats listed in this book offer broad categories, and you can use this information to understand more about a plant's needs, but it's a fascinating experiment to dig deeper into the various types of habitats found naturally in your specific locale and to learn about the plants growing there.

RANGE: Just as each plant has a native habitat, it also has a native range and, again, one can get increasingly specific in designating this range. I've stuck to the broad categories of northeast (which runs roughly from New England and the Great Lakes east to the Atlantic coast), prairies (which goes from the U.S. midwest and Canadian prairies – including a tiny tip of southwestern Ontario – west to the great plains), and the northwest (which includes the Rocky Mountains west to the Pacific coast, from the middle of Oregon north through British Columbia). For gardeners wishing to include only those natives that existed in their local area prior to European settlement, you'll need to delve deeper than these broad categories allow (indeed,

you'll almost need a field guide written for your town or city – which is not as difficult to find as it sounds; many local naturalist groups have compiled just such lists, so contact local nature groups or university botany departments for good places to start your hunt). Field guides such as Peterson's or Audubon's are also indispensable tools for information about a plant's native range.

You'll note that one piece of conventional gardening information not found in this book is any reference to zones. In the native plant garden, the zone system is all but irrelevant; it's replaced with knowledge about a plant's native habitat and native range. Once you determine that a plant is native to your area, you'll know without doubt that it is hardy in your zone.

DESCRIPTION: There's always a lot more, of course, to say about each plant, but I've tried to include those features noteworthy for a garden setting. My biases – an insatiable desire for blue, a consistent affection for leguminous plants, a willingness to indulge an invasive native's urge to take over – are on the table, so if your preferences run to yellow, controlled growers of the non-leguminous variety, you'll at least know the context for my enthusiasms.

MAINTENANCE AND REQUIREMENTS: I recently read a review of a gardening book in which the author was praised for going beyond the shopworn phrases (such as "needs good drainage and loamy soil") and instead providing "more useful" details such as "needs soil that is 47.3% sand, 29.8% loam, 22.9% clay; prefers a north-facing slope at a 33.7-degree angle, with a 23-mile-an-hour wind buffeting the plant in morning and dead calm at night." Okay, I exaggerate. While such specificity may well have been necessary for the plants detailed in that book (just try growing the non-native Himalayan blue poppy, for example, without Virgo-ish attention to detail) and while I support and applaud such specificity, those "shopworn" phrases are in fact more than adequate for the plants listed in this book. For the most part, the easy-to-grow natives included here aren't the least bit fussy or demanding. Sure, some require acidic soil, some require a lot of moisture, but beyond that, take the "easy" part to heart; as long as you follow the general suggestions outlined in the listing, you don't need to worry.

Propagation: I'm lazy and I don't have an inch of workspace, so I tend to buy or trade most of my plants (I confess, it's often a one-way trade, to my benefit – luckily, I've got generous and forgiving gardening buddies). But whenever I've experimented with seed-starting, I've been amazed and gratified by the results. Little is more satisfying than nurturing a tiny seed to maturity, and it's a logical next step for gardeners exploring the world of native plants. For starters, it's easier to find more uncommon natives as seeds than as plants for sale at the nursery. (You can find them through seed exchanges, such as the North American Native Plant Society's, or by carefully harvesting a sustainable amount of common seed from a healthy and large wild population.) But beyond that, there's also the satisfaction of knowing that you're nurturing the genetic diversity seeds provide (as opposed to the clonal propagation methods of cuttings, for example, which grow as genetically identical to the parent plant). Almost all of the plants listed here are easy to start from seeds; for those that aren't, an easy alternative method of propagation is provided. For more information on propagation methods, see page 137, which gives step-by-step instructions and explains some of the propagation terms used in the listings. And to ensure that your seed-collecting from wild populations is sustainable, see the North American Native Plant Society's Ethical Gardener's Guidelines, on page 136.

Good Companions: All of the plant combinations listed are ones that I've seen in gardens and enjoyed. It's a subjective list, of course, and the options are endless, so experiment! I've included as good companions some plants that are not detailed in this book; for more information on these plants, consult a field guide.

Related Species: Some plants (false Solomon's seal and nodding wild onion, to name just two) have a very broad native range, growing across the continent; most others have a more restricted range. However, a plant with a range restricted to the prairies, for example, often has many related species (i.e., in the same genus) in other regions. So if you're a northeast gardener and you like the look of the gorgeous satin flower, native to the northwest, look in the entry under "Related Species" for related plants in your region. In this way, although the title says 100, and there are in fact 101, actually, there are hundreds!

Wildlife: When you garden with native plants, you're automatically gardening for wildlife too.

Native plants and animals have evolved together over millennia, and many symbiotic, complex, perhaps even unknowable relationships have developed over that time. When we mess around with wild plant species, hybridizing them for bigger flowers, for example, we're also messing around with the plant's pollinating insect, whose mouth parts may have evolved exactly to fit the shape of the wild species. And when we banish milkweeds from the garden, branding them noxious weeds, we're also banishing monarch butterflies, for whom milkweeds are the only known larval food. Politics aside, plant natives and the birds, butterflies, and insects will find your garden. (All of the meadow and prairie plants, in particular, are great for attracting butterflies. I've included the noteworthy species in the listings.)

Since our culture tends to insect-phobia (and the associated chemical controls), it's important to note that by far the vast majority of insects you attract to the garden are beneficial – pollinating plants, feeding the birds, eating other pests, and so on.

MISCELLANY: A catch-all category for tidbits.

100 Easy-to-Grow
Native Plants

Old stumps and dead trees provide habitat for wildlife in the garden – they quickly become attractive design features as well. In this northeastern woodland garden, foamflower (*Tiarella cordifolia*) surrounds a stump, which is bursting with the volunteer growth of creeping phlox (*Phlox stolonifera*).

BARREN STRAWBERRY

Waldsteinia fragarioides

Barren strawberry (background) with foamflower (foreground)

HEIGHT: 3–8 inches (8–20 cm)
BLOOMING PERIOD: spring to early summer
EXPOSURE: partial shade to filtered sun
MOISTURE: average to dry
HABITAT: woods and clearings
RANGE: northeast and prairies

DESCRIPTION: I'm always on a desperate hunt for attractive woodland groundcovers that do well in dry conditions, and barren strawberry delivers. Its evergreen basal leaves are divided into three leaflets (like strawberry plants, but rounder) and the plant spreads well, covering the ground quickly. Flowers are prolific, with many in a cluster, and bright yellow. The glossy leaves brighten up a shady woodland corner.

MAINTENANCE AND REQUIREMENTS: Barren strawberry prefers soil that's high in organic matter, on the slightly acidic side, but other than that, it's not fussy. You can grow it either in partial shade or in more open, dappled light conditions.

PROPAGATION: Start from seeds or divide plants in spring or fall. It spreads rapidly from underground stolons.

GOOD COMPANIONS: In acidic conditions, plant with wintergreen (*Gaultheria procumbens*), a creeping evergreen with white bell-shaped flowers in spring. It also looks good with foamflower (*Tiarella cordifolia*), wild ginger (*Asarum canadense*), wild blue phlox (*Phlox divaricata*), twinleaf (*Jeffersonia diphylla*), and Christmas fern (*Polystichum acrostichoides*).

MISCELLANY: Although the name is strawberry, "barren" is a clue: no edible berries, alas.

BEE BALM

Monarda didyma

HEIGHT: 2–5 feet (60–150 cm)	**MOISTURE:** moist to average
BLOOMING PERIOD: early to mid-summer	**HABITAT:** moist woods, moist meadows
EXPOSURE: partial shade to full sun	**RANGE:** northeast

DESCRIPTION: Striking red flowers that look like jesters' hats and last for weeks give this plant a slightly comical air. Its stem is square (characteristic of plants in the mint family) and its leaves are dark green, sometimes flushed with dark red. Quickly growing into a large, tall clump, bee balm is altogether a sturdy, colorful addition to the garden.

MAINTENANCE AND REQUIREMENTS: Although bee balm prefers moist places in the wild, it can be grown in average moisture conditions in the garden. Versatile in its light requirements, from partial shade to full sun, and also in its pH tolerance, from slightly acidic to neutral (pH 5.5 to 6.5), bee balm is very easy to grow. The only problem you may encounter is mold, which often covers the leaves in a whitish film, signaling that the plant is crowded and not getting enough air movement; divide plants every few years, and don't spray leaves when watering. Deadhead to extend blooming.

PROPAGATION: Bee balm is easy to start from seeds. Simply sprinkle seeds in pots or a bed in late fall or early spring (seeds do not need cold stratification). Or divide the plant in early spring, which is not only useful for propagation, but also helps keep the plant from getting too crowded in the center.

GOOD COMPANIONS: At the woodland edge, plant bee balm with black-eyed Susan (*Rudbeckia hirta*) and woodland sunflower (*Helianthus divaricatus*).

RELATED SPECIES: See entry for wild bergamot (*M. fistulosa*).

WILDLIFE: Bees, butterflies, and hummingbirds swarm this plant for nectar.

MISCELLANY: Also known as Oswego tea, because the plants were used by the Oswego Indians for a hot drink. Bruise its aromatic leaves for the scent of Earl Grey tea.

BIG BLUESTEM

Andropogon gerardii

HEIGHT: 3–8 feet (.9–2.4 m)
BLOOMING PERIOD: late summer
EXPOSURE: full sun

MOISTURE: moist to dry; drought tolerant
HABITAT: prairies, meadows
RANGE: tallgrass and mixed-grass prairies

DESCRIPTION: We don't often take note of grass flowers, but with big bluestem, it's the flowers that give the plant its characteristic "turkey foot" at the top of the stems in late summer. Clump-forming and very tall-growing, the whole plant has a bluish cast in summer, then turns bronze in fall. Although you can grow it as an attractive specimen plant (that is, singly as a focal point), big bluestem is made to dominate large areas, punctuated with tall-growing wildflowers such as prairie dock (*Silphium terebinthinaceum*).

MAINTENANCE AND REQUIREMENTS: Big bluestem is a versatile grass, growing in moist, average, and dry soils, acidic to neutral conditions, clay to sandier soils. It is extremely drought tolerant and can even grow in light shade.

PROPAGATION: Easy to start from seeds, which mature in late fall. Don't worry if there's not a lot of top growth the first year, as the plant is busy building up its massive root system.

GOOD COMPANIONS: Combines nicely with Indian grass (*Sorghastrum nutans*) and the dramatically tall prairie plants, such as the silphiums (see entries for compass plant and cup plant), tall sunflower (*Helianthus giganteus*), and tall coreopsis (*Coreopsis tripteris*).

RELATED SPECIES: Little bluestem (*A. scoparius*), which grows 1 1/2 to 4 1/2 feet (45 to 135 cm) and turns reddish gold in fall, is a good alternative for smaller gardens (so there's no reason not to include at least *some* grasses in your meadow or prairie planting) – along with the grace grasses provide, the birds will appreciate the seeds.

WILDLIFE: Attracts birds and butterflies (many butterflies, such as the skippers and wood nymphs, lay their eggs on native prairie grasses).

BLACK-EYED SUSAN

Rudbeckia hirta

HEIGHT: 1–3 feet (30–90 cm)	**MOISTURE:** average to dry; drought tolerant
BLOOMING PERIOD: summer to fall	**HABITAT:** dry meadows, prairies, open woods
EXPOSURE: full sun to partial sun	**RANGE:** northeast and prairies

DESCRIPTION: Surely one of the most cheerful and popular of the native wildflowers, black-eyed Susan is a must in the meadow or prairie garden. Its prolific, long-lasting blooms – yellow with dark centers – and its ease of cultivation make it a rewarding plant. If you want a less common species, try any of the related rudbeckias listed below – all are equally easy and versatile. Although often listed as a biennial, black-eyed Susan will behave as a perennial if it's happy and an annual if it's not.

MAINTENANCE AND REQUIREMENTS: Black-eyed Susan thrives in tough conditions – in sandy or gravelly, nutrient-poor soil and long periods of drought. Don't supplement the soil with fertilizer or organic material such as compost before planting, as you don't want the soil to be too rich (resulting in fewer blooms and weaker stems). Acidic to neutral soil, clay to sand.

PROPAGATION: Easy to start from seeds, which ripen in fall, or divide mature plants in early spring or in fall.

GOOD COMPANIONS: Black-eyed Susan looks great with almost any of the native prairie and meadow species, but I particularly like it with airy white flowers such as flowering spurge (*Euphorbia corollata*) and pearly everlasting (*Anaphalis margaritacea*), and with the brilliant orange of butterfly weed (*Asclepias tuberosa*) or the deep blue-purple of *Delphinium exaltatum*.

RELATED SPECIES: Brown-eyed Susan (*R. triloba*) just showed up in my dry, open woodland garden one summer and has been spreading ever since. Its flowers are smaller but more abundant than *R. hirta* and the whole plant is bushier, with many branches. Sweet black-eyed Susan (*R. subtomentosa*) is much taller, to 6 feet (1.8 m). Green-headed coneflower (*R. laciniata*) is also very tall (3 to 8 feet/.9 to 2.4 m) and grows in the open shade of woodlands or in sun, blooming in summer.

WILDLIFE: Nectar attracts butterflies and bees.

BLACK SNAKEROOT

Cimicifuga racemosa

Black snakeroot (right) with cup plant (left)

HEIGHT: 3–8 feet (.9–2.4 m)	**MOISTURE:** average
BLOOMING PERIOD: summer	**HABITAT:** rich woods
EXPOSURE: deep shade to filtered light	**RANGE:** northeast and prairies

DESCRIPTION: Just what the woodland garden needs – a dramatic and showy flower in summer, after the dramatic and showy spring bloomers have done their bit. Black snakeroot sends up startlingly tall wands covered in white flowers – these swaying wands dappled with filtered light make a truly dazzling sight. Black snakeroot is also very effective as a reliable foliage plant, as it gets large and bushy. Its leaves are sharply toothed and twice divided into threes, and for the life of me I can barely distinguish them from red or white baneberry (*Actaea pachypoda* or *A. rubra*).

MAINTENANCE AND REQUIREMENTS: Give black snakeroot humus-rich woodland soil in full shade to dappled light and it will thrive. Mine does just fine in very dry woodland soil and is even spreading, though after four years it has yet to bloom (an unusually long post-transplant delay for this species). Prefers acidic to slightly acidic soil.

PROPAGATION: Seeds ripen in autumn, and young plants will take a few years to flower. Plants can also be divided in spring or fall.

GOOD COMPANIONS: A nice groundcover to plant around black snakeroot is the semi-evergreen green-and-gold (*Chrysogonum virginianum*). It also looks good with meadowrue (*Thalictrum polygamum*), fairy bells (*Disporum lanuginosum*), Christmas fern (*Polystichum acrostichoides*), and maidenhair fern (*Adiantum pedatum*).

RELATED SPECIES: In the northwest, the related tall bugbane (*C. elata*), also known as black cohosh, is a rare plant and thus is not found in the nursery trade.

WILDLIFE: Black snakeroot is a larval food plant for the spring azure butterfly.

MISCELLANY: Also known as bugbane and black cohosh (blue cohosh, a northeastern woodland native, is *Caulophyllum thalictroides*).

BLOODROOT

Sanguinaria canadensis

HEIGHT: 10 inches (25 cm)	**MOISTURE:** moist to average
BLOOMING PERIOD: early spring	**HABITAT:** deciduous woods
	RANGE: northeast and prairies
EXPOSURE: shade	

DESCRIPTION: There's no surer sign of spring taking hold than the appearance of bloodroot's cheerful white flowers. Although the blooms don't last long, and are easily de-petalled by wind, this little charmer is a northeastern woodland garden must. The leaves clasp the stem, all lined up like a sentry, and slowly unfurl to reveal large, saucer-shaped but deeply scalloped foliage. Effective as a groundcover, especially around the base of trees.

MAINTENANCE AND REQUIREMENTS: Give bloodroot rich, moist woodland soil, semi-acidic to neutral (pH 5.5 to 6.5), and it will flourish, spreading into groundcovering colonies. During mid-summer dry periods, though, it will start to yellow and may even go dormant, so mulch to conserve moisture.

PROPAGATION: Sow seeds immediately upon ripening (approximately one month after flowering). Mature seeds are spilled quickly by the plant, so you may want to place a small bag over the seed capsule to catch them. Or divide rhizomes when the plant is dormant, in early spring or in fall – you'll notice the roots' red juice, from which the plant gets its name.

GOOD COMPANIONS: In deep shade, combine with wild ginger (*Asarum canadense*), blue cohosh (*Caulophyllum thalictroides*), Canada violet (*Viola canadensis*), squirrel corn (*Dicentra canadensis*), and goldenseal (*Hydrastis canadensis*). In filtered shade, try interplanting with columbine (*Aquilegia canadensis*) – the taller red flowers of columbine will rise above the low-growing bloodroot.

WILDLIFE: Bloodroot seeds are dispersed by ants.

After a burst of spring color, the northeastern woodland garden provides a cool green retreat in summer.
Above the stump is twisted stalk (*Streptopus amplexifolius*). From lower right to left: sharp-lobed hepatica
(*Hepatica acutiloba*), Solomon's seal (*Polygonatum biflorum*), and wild ginger (*Asarum canadense*).
The starry leaves in the middle left are the non-native sweet woodruff (*Galium odoratum*).

Blue vervain (middle) with boneset (left)

BLUE VERVAIN

Verbena hastata

HEIGHT: 3–5 feet (90–150 cm)	**MOISTURE:** moist to average
BLOOMING PERIOD: mid- to late summer	**HABITAT:** damp thickets, wet meadows
EXPOSURE: full sun to partial sun	**RANGE:** prairies and northeast

DESCRIPTION: Vervain is one of my favorite plants for sunny meadow and prairie gardens; there's something so perky but understated about it. Spikes of purple-blue flowers appear in mid-summer and continue blooming for weeks (even flowering again if you deadhead plants). Though the flowers are small, they're attractive, and the spikes, even after blooming, provide interest. Blooms start opening at the bottom of the spike and progress upwards.

MAINTENANCE AND REQUIREMENTS: In the wild, vervain grows in wet meadows and ditches, so it definitely prefers moisture. However, I grow mine in dry soil that is never watered (except by rain) and it thrives. Deadhead to extend blooming, but other than that, vervain requires no special care. It may get a white mold on the leaves if the plant is crowded or stressed, but the mold won't kill the plant (divide the plant to increase air circulation). Can be aggressive.

PROPAGATION: Vervain is a prodigious self-seeder, even popping up in the cracks between bricks in my garden. Very easy to start from seeds, which ripen in late summer or early fall.

GOOD COMPANIONS: I think vervain goes with everything. Particularly attractive companions include Virginia mountain mint (*Pycnanthemum virginianum*), evening primrose (*Oenothera biennis*), false sunflower (*Heliopsis helianthoides*), daisy fleabane (*Erigeron annuus*), and wild indigo (*Baptisia tinctoria*).

RELATED SPECIES: Hoary vervain (*V. stricta*) has plumper-looking flowers and the leaves are rounder.

WILDLIFE: Attracts bees; nectar plant for butterflies.

BONESET

Eupatorium perfoliatum

Boneset (bottom right) with Joe-pye weed (left)

HEIGHT: 2–5 feet (60–150 cm)
BLOOMING PERIOD: mid-summer to autumn
EXPOSURE: full sun
MOISTURE: moist to average
HABITAT: wet meadows
RANGE: prairies and northeast

DESCRIPTION: The leaves of boneset are rather coarse, surrounding the stem and growing straight out, horizontally; they're rough, hairy, and sort of crinkly. But the flowers are very attractive: large clusters of long-lasting white blooms from summer through to autumn. Boneset looks especially good near the back of the border, in a big clump. Its strong stems never flop and thus it can be used to support weaker-stemmed growers, such as heath aster (*Aster ericoides*) and sky blue aster (*A. azureus*).

MAINTENANCE AND REQUIREMENTS: Boneset prefers moist conditions but will do just fine in average soil, as long as it gets sun. Give it lots of room as it will fill in large areas to dramatic effect. Adaptable in its nutrient needs and pH.

PROPAGATION: Start from seeds, which mature in autumn and are very small (sow them on the surface of soil as they require light to germinate), or divide clumps in spring or fall.

GOOD COMPANIONS: Boneset is a knockout with spotted Joe-pye weed (*Eupatorium maculatum*), the fall-blooming asters, such as New England aster (*Aster novae-angliae*), and stiff goldenrod (*Solidago rigida*).

RELATED SPECIES: See entry for spotted Joe-pye weed (*E. maculatum*).

WILDLIFE: Attracts nectar-seeking butterflies.

MISCELLANY: The leaves of this plant were sometimes used to wrap around splints, to help bones heal – hence, the common name.

BOTTLEBRUSH GRASS

Hystrix patula

HEIGHT: 4–5 feet (1.2–1.5 m)	**HABITAT:** woods, open clearings
BLOOMING PERIOD: summer	
EXPOSURE: partial shade	**RANGE:** prairies and northeast
MOISTURE: moist to dry	

DESCRIPTION: Although it's unusual to see grass-like plants in the woodland garden, there *are* a number of grasses, sedges, and other grass-like species that do well in shade and should be considered by gardeners looking for something a bit different. Bottlebrush grass is particularly stunning when its gorgeous bristly seedheads (yes, in a bottlebrush shape) are touched by filtered sun.

MAINTENANCE AND REQUIREMENTS: Bottlebrush grass does best in well-drained woodland soil, in the partial shade provided by a high canopy cover. Give it room to spread into a large stand.

PROPAGATION: Start from seeds, which ripen in late summer.

GOOD COMPANIONS: Bottlebrush grass does well with any of the woodland species that grow in filtered light, such as tall meadowrue (*Thalictrum polygamum*). I also like to see it with black snakeroot (*Cimicifuga racemosa*) for a dramatic combination of flowering spikes.

MISCELLANY: The genus name, *Hystrix*, is from the Greek for hedgehog, attesting to the spikey look of this grass.

BOTTLE GENTIAN

Gentiana andrewsii

HEIGHT: 1–2 feet (30–60 cm)
BLOOMING PERIOD: late summer to fall
EXPOSURE: full sun to filtered sun
MOISTURE: moist to average
HABITAT: wet meadows, prairies, open woods
RANGE: prairies and northeast

DESCRIPTION: Here's a blue to make the spirits soar . . . and a wonderfully weird shape to boot. Bottle gentian has an awful lot going for it, not the least of which is that it blooms just when things are winding down in the garden in late summer and when you've really had enough of yellow flowers, thank you very much. Just then, the brilliant blue and elongated blobs of bottle gentian appear and cheer things up. Put it somewhere close to the front of the border, so it doesn't get overwhelmed.

MAINTENANCE AND REQUIREMENTS: Although in the wild bottle gentian grows in wet meadows, it will do fine in average soil moisture, in sun to filtered light. But if you do have a moist spot, near a downspout for instance, put it there and let it naturalize. Does well in average to rich soil, acidic to neutral.

PROPAGATION: Plant gentian's fine seeds on the soil's surface in late fall. Plants can also be divided in spring. Happily, bottle gentian spreads well on its own – not aggressively, but steadily.

GOOD COMPANIONS: I think you can't beat bottle gentian all on its own; it needs no companions, which will just distract from it. That said, it does look great with white turtlehead (*Chelone glabra*) and grass of Parnassus (*Parnassia glauca*), both of which prefer wet soils and filtered light, and bloom in late summer.

RELATED SPECIES: Difficult to find in the nursery trade, but available through seed exchanges, is fringed gentian (*G. crinita*), which is also brilliantly blue but with fringed petals rather than closed "bottles"; native to the northeast and prairie regions. A gentian for dry prairies is the biennial downy gentian (*G. puberulenta*), with cup-shaped blue flowers. In the northwest, try big gentian (*G. sceptrum*), broad-petalled gentian (*G. platypetala*), or *G. calycosa*, but only if you have very moist conditions.

Broad-leaved shooting star (left) with white fawn lily (right)

BROAD-LEAVED SHOOTING STAR

Dodecatheon hendersonii

HEIGHT: 3–20 inches (8–50 cm)
BLOOMING PERIOD: spring
EXPOSURE: partial sun to shade
MOISTURE: moist to dry; drought tolerant in summer
HABITAT: meadows, open woods
RANGE: northwest and Rocky Mountains

DESCRIPTION: Shooting star gets my vote as one of the most playful-looking flowers around – silly and enchanting at the same time. It looks as if dropped out of the sky, a bright magenta marauder, with yellow at the base. Flowers appear in spring and last for weeks. The oval leaves hug the ground. Good for use in a rock garden, meadow garden, or open woodland.

MAINTENANCE AND REQUIREMENTS: Give it rich soil with good drainage in partial sun to shade. After blooming, it's fine if the soil dries out, as shooting star is adapted to summer drought.

PROPAGATION: Start from seeds, which ripen in summer and are often slow to germinate, or divide in autumn.

GOOD COMPANIONS: Shooting star looks good with miner's lettuce (*Montia sibirica*) and trillium (*Trillium ovatum*). Another stellar combo is shooting star and white fawn lily (*Erythronium oregonum*). For foliage contrast, plant with wood sorrel (*Oxalis oregana*).

RELATED SPECIES: In the northwest, also try few-flowered shooting star (*D. pulchellum*), which prefers moist soil in partial shade and requires good drainage. Prairie and northeastern species include *D. meadia*, which has pink flowers and grows up to 2 feet (60 cm) in open woods and prairies; prefers neutral soil.

MISCELLANY: Shooting stars are often wild-dug, so make sure the plant is nursery propagated.

BROAD-LEAVED STONECROP

Sedum spathulifolium

HEIGHT: 3–8 inches (8–20 cm)	**MOISTURE:** dry to moist; drought tolerant
BLOOMING PERIOD: spring to early summer	**HABITAT:** rocky outcrops
EXPOSURE: full to partial sun	**RANGE:** northwest

DESCRIPTION: Yellow star-like flowers appear in spring, atop thick, glaucous basal leaves. The plant's flat rosettes are often red-tinged in sun. Broad-leaved stonecrop is great as a spreading groundcover in rock gardens and on very dry sites. Try growing it in a rock wall, where its flowers will spill out of crevasses.

MAINTENANCE AND REQUIREMENTS: Stonecrop is one of those wonderfully forgiving plants – it actually prefers very dry, nutrient-poor, thin soils. Hence, it's great for problem areas, as long as it gets some sun.

PROPAGATION: Stem cuttings readily root.

GOOD COMPANIONS: A low-maintenance but colorful combination includes salal (*Gaultheria shallon*), nodding onion (*Allium cernuum*), and camas (*Camassia quamash*).

RELATED SPECIES: In the northwest, try roseroot (*S. integrifolium*), with pink and dark purple flowers, and Oregon stonecrop (*S. oreganum*), with yellow flowers – both are evergreen, mat-forming succulents found on open, rocky sites, and both require full sun and well-drained soil. In the northeast, try wild stonecrop (*S. ternatum*), which does well in shade in rich, moist soil and has whitish star-shaped flowers in spring. In the prairies, try narrow-petaled stonecrop (*S. stenopetalum*), with its succulent gray-green leaves and yellow flowers in early summer.

Dried seedheads of golden alexanders (*Zizia aurea*) poke up from a clump of black-eyed Susan (*Rudbeckia hirta*), with the tall wand of liatris (*Liatris pycnostachya*) completing this elegant prairie combination.

BUTTERFLY WEED

Asclepias tuberosa

HEIGHT: 2–3 feet (60–90 cm)	**MOISTURE:** dry to average;
BLOOMING PERIOD:	drought tolerant
mid-summer	**HABITAT:** prairies and meadows
EXPOSURE: full sun to light	**RANGE:** prairies and northeast
shade	

DESCRIPTION: For an electric highlight of orange in the sunny garden, you can't beat butterfly weed – plus, it's one of the top butterfly-attracting plants around. Clusters of orange flowers are borne at the top of 2- to 3-foot (60 to 90 cm) stems; leaves are narrow and dark green. Plants get bushy if they've got lots of room and, if crowded, stay narrow, straining for the sun. The seed pods are also very striking, large pods (4 to 5 inches/10 to 12.5 cm).

MAINTENANCE AND REQUIREMENTS: Butterfly weed prefers well-drained soil and will tolerate a broad range of conditions, from sand to clay slightly acid to neutral soil. Don't let young seedlings dry out, but once established, plants are very drought tolerant. Butterfly weed emerges quite late in spring, so be careful not to cultivate around it, as it doesn't like disturbance.

PROPAGATION: Easy to start from seeds, which mature in autumn. When seedlings are of transplantable size, place them in their permanent home, as butterfly weed's long taproot resents being moved. You can also divide rootstalk in early spring or fall.

GOOD COMPANIONS: Butterfly weed looks wonderful with almost any summer-blooming prairie natives, especially blazing star (*Liatris* spp.), prairie phlox (*Phlox pilosa*), and leadplant (*Amorpha canescens*), but for something a bit different, try planting it at the edge of a woodland garden, in a place where it will get sun. Also looks great with June grass (*Koeleria cristata*), which grows in clumps 1 to 2 feet (30 to 60 cm) tall and has fuzzy, spiky seedheads.

RELATED SPECIES: Though the common milkweed (*A. syriaca*) is a much-maligned plant, many of the milkweed species are not only very controlled plants, but are also very good candidates for prairie and northeastern gardens. One of the most graceful is whorled milkweed (*A. verticillata*), which has very slender leaves and airy clusters of small white flowers for many weeks in summer. See also the entry for swamp milkweed (*A. incarnata*).

WILDLIFE: Milkweeds are the larval host plant for the monarch butterfly and also the queen butterfly. Their nectar attracts many other butterfly species and bees.

CAMAS

Camassia quamash

HEIGHT: 1–2 feet (30–60 cm)	**MOISTURE:** moist to average; summer-drought tolerant
BLOOMING PERIOD: spring	**HABITAT:** meadows
EXPOSURE: sun to partial sun	**RANGE:** northwest

DESCRIPTION: You can't beat the glowing blues of camas's tall flowers – star-shaped along the spike, with yellow centers. Grass-like leaves, which look a bit like daffodil leaves, are also elegant. For a stunning show, plant camas bulbs throughout the lawn. (Or better yet, ditch the lawn and plant a meadow!) If you have Garry oaks on your property, camas is a must – and is the beginning of a Garry oak meadow garden (see Good Companions section at right).

MAINTENANCE AND REQUIREMENTS: Although camas prefers moist soil in spring, it's naturally adapted to summer drought, so don't do any supplementary watering for this plant. If you're growing it in a grassy meadow or lawn, don't cut or mow until mid-summer, after the seeds have set. Camas does well in heavy soil.

PROPAGATION: Seeds should be sown fresh in mid-summer; plants will take approximately four years to flower from seed. Camas can also be propagated from bulbils, which grow slowly along the mature bulbs.

GOOD COMPANIONS: Meadow species to grow with camas include blue-eyed Mary (*Collinsia parviflora*), broad-leaved shooting star (*Dodecatheon hendersonii*), satin flower (*Sisyrinchium douglasii*), white fawn lily (*Erythronium oregonum*), miner's lettuce (*Montia sibirica*), harvest brodiaea (*Brodiaea coronaria*), and chocolate lily (*Fritillaria lanceolata*). Native meadow grasses include Idaho fescue (*Festuca idahoensis*) and western fescue (*Festuca occidentalis*).

RELATED SPECIES: In the midwest to northeast, try eastern camas (*Camassia scilloides*). Native to damp meadows, prairies, and open woodlands, it has blue to lavender flowers and grows 1 to 2 feet (30 to 60 cm).

CANADA ANEMONE

Anemone canadensis

HEIGHT: 1–2 feet (30–60 cm)	**MOISTURE:** moist to average
BLOOMING PERIOD: late spring to early summer	**HABITAT:** moist meadows, open woods
EXPOSURE: full sun to partial sun	**RANGE:** prairies and northeast

DESCRIPTION: Canada anemone is a vigorous, aggressive grower in moist sites, full to partial sun, but somewhat less invasive in average soil conditions. (I grow mine in the dry, partial shade of a Norway maple; while it doesn't bloom well, probably because it's crowded, it provides a reliable green under those difficult conditions.) Its small (1 inch/2.5 cm) single white flowers with yellow centers appear at the top of the stem in late spring and last into early summer. Although a mass of Canada anemone in bloom is a stunning site, I almost prefer it just before the flowers open, when its round whitish buds are like small white dots, punctuating the dark green of the leaves.

MAINTENANCE AND REQUIREMENTS: Because of its aggressive nature, plant Canada anemone in a spot where it can run rampant – along a moist bank, for example. It flourishes in moist soil, but will do just fine in regular soil; neutral pH.

PROPAGATION: It's easy to grow Canada anemone from seeds, which ripen in early summer. Or just leave the plant on its own to spread via its underground rhizomes.

GOOD COMPANIONS: In moist areas, plant with blue flag (*Iris versicolor*) for a striking combination of blue and white. Also works well with dogbane (*Amsonia tabernaemontana*) and meadowsweet (*Spiraea latifolia*).

RELATED SPECIES: For the northeast and prairie regions, thimbleweed (*A. cylindrica*) has a similar flower and leaf shape, but a much more interesting seedhead – a tall, cylindrical "thimble"; prefers dry conditions and is drought tolerant. Tall anemone (*A. virginiana*) grows in open woodlands; wood anemone (*A. quinquefolia*) is a great woodland groundcover, grows 4 to 8 inches (10 to 20 cm) in open shade, and has white blooms in spring. For northwest species, see the entry for pasque flower (*A. patens*).

CANADA MAYFLOWER

Maianthemum dilatatum

HEIGHT: 6–8 inches (15–20 cm)	**MOISTURE:** average to moist
BLOOMING PERIOD: spring to summer	**HABITAT:** woods
EXPOSURE: deep shade to partial shade	**RANGE:** northwest

DESCRIPTION: Canada mayflower is the groundcover of choice in deeply shady, acidic, nutrient-poor sites – a trying combination. Low-growing, it spreads to carpet the ground with its glossy, often curled, heart-shaped leaves, and in spring through summer, it sends up dainty, white, star-shaped flowers in cylindrical clusters. Red berries in summer are also a nice feature.

MAINTENANCE AND REQUIREMENTS: A versatile plant, Canada mayflower will grow in deep to partial shade, average to summer-dry soil, as long as conditions are slightly to strongly acidic.

PROPAGATION: Plant seeds fresh (when berries turn red), in late summer, or divide rhizomes in spring or fall, which is a much faster method of propagation.

GOOD COMPANIONS: In the northwest, an effortless but pleasing combination includes Canada mayflower, bunchberry (*Cornus canadensis*), deer fern (*Blechnum spicant*), and trillium (*Trillium ovatum*). Also looks great with sword fern (*Polystichum munitum*) and false Solomon's seal (*Smilacina racemosa*).

RELATED SPECIES: A closely related species, *M. canadense*, grows in woods and clearings in the northeast and prairie regions and is an excellent groundcover.

MISCELLANY: Sometimes called false lily of the valley, though not related to the non-native lily of the valley (*Convallaria majalis*).

CANADA MILK VETCH

Astragalus canadensis

HEIGHT: 2–4 feet (60–120 cm)	**MOISTURE:** average to dry
BLOOMING PERIOD: summer	**HABITAT:** thickets, prairies
EXPOSURE: full sun to partial sun	**RANGE:** prairies and northeast

DESCRIPTION: If, like me, you think that lupines are almost perfect plants, you'll also love Canada milk vetch. Leaves are pinnate and smooth; flowers are lupine-like and creamy white, in showy elongated clusters at the end of a stalk. Milk vetch is a nitrogen-fixing plant and produces the hard seed pods characteristic of legumes.

MAINTENANCE AND REQUIREMENTS: Nothing much to worry about with Canada milk vetch, although you may need to stake up the plant (but I like the way it gets sort of rangy and free-flowing).

PROPAGATION: Easy to start from seeds, which mature in late summer (shake them out of the hard pod). If you're collecting seeds from established plants, take a bit of the surrounding soil and use some in your starter pots, as the soil will contain the rhizobium (microorganisms that live in association with the roots of nitrogen-fixing legumes) required for germination. If purchasing seeds, ask for astragalus-type rhizobium.

GOOD COMPANIONS: For a nice contrast of flower and leaf shape, plant with nodding onion (*Allium cernuum*). Wild petunia (*Ruellia humilis*), with its gorgeous purple flowers, is also a good companion, as are purple prairie clover (*Petalostemum purpureum*) and false sunflower (*Heliopsis helianthoides*).

RELATED SPECIES: There are many beautiful milk vetches native to the tallgrass region. Try the deep purple flowered two-grooved milk vetch (*A. bisulcatus*), which blooms in early summer and grows up to 2 feet (60 cm), or the white-flowered Drummond's milk vetch (*A. drummondii*), which has hairy gray-green leaves and grows up to 3 feet (90 cm). Wooly locoweed (*A. mollissimus*) is low growing (to 18 inches/45 cm) and bushy and has spikes of violet flowers in early summer. In the northwest, particularly in a rock garden, try *A. kentrophyta*, which has blue flowers.

WILDLIFE: Attracts birds, butterflies, and hummingbirds. Larval host plant for western tailed blue butterfly.

This informal meadow planting requires little ongoing care, as purple coneflower (*Echinacea purpurea*) virtually looks after itself.

CANADA WILD RYE

Elymus canadensis

HEIGHT: 3–5 feet (.9–1.5 m)
BLOOMING PERIOD: summer
EXPOSURE: full to partial sun
MOISTURE: moist to dry;
   drought tolerant

HABITAT: prairies and meadows
RANGE: tallgrass, mixed-grass,
   and shortgrass prairies and
   northeast

DESCRIPTION: If you've got a large bare area that you eventually want to return to prairie and you want to cover the soil quickly so weeds can't grow, Canada wild rye is a great groundcovering grass to plant while you're waiting for slower-growing species to get established. Flowers (a bushy inflorescence) are very showy – 4 to 10 inches (10 to 25 cm) long and looking almost like wheat. Seed plumes turn gold as they ripen, nodding under their weight. A delicate-looking, airy plant, but extraordinarily tough.

MAINTENANCE AND REQUIREMENTS: Canada wild rye is extremely versatile, growing in pretty well all soil types, from clay to sand, moist to dry, acidic to neutral. Requires no maintenance whatsoever.

PROPAGATION: Easy to start from seeds, which mature in late summer and in fall.

GOOD COMPANIONS: For an ornamental planting, combine with butterfly weed (*Asclepias tuberosa*), white false indigo (*Baptisia leucantha*), which produces creamy white flower clusters in early summer and grows 3 to 5 feet (90 to 150 cm), and prairie phlox (*Phlox pilosa*), which has lavender flower clusters in early summer and grows 1 to 2 feet (30 to 60 cm).

RELATED SPECIES: In the northwest, try blue wild rye (*E. glaucus*), which grows 2 to 3 feet (60 to 90 cm).

CARDINAL FLOWER

Lobelia cardinalis

HEIGHT: 2–4 feet (60–120 cm)
BLOOMING PERIOD: mid- to late summer
EXPOSURE: full sun to partial shade
MOISTURE: moist to wet
HABITAT: wet meadows
RANGE: prairies and northeast

DESCRIPTION: There is perhaps no more striking red to be found in the garden than that of cardinal flower – so named after the bright robes worn by Roman Catholic cardinals. The brilliant tubular flowers extend along an erect stalk and last for weeks. Leaves are toothed, dark green, and an attractive foil for the flowers. Perfect for moist sites, along the edges of a stream, or where downspouts drain into the soil. It's particularly attractive when planted at the edge of a woodland garden.

MAINTENANCE AND REQUIREMENTS: Moisture is the main requirement for cardinal flower – the soil cannot be allowed to dry out or the plant will most likely die. Give it nutrient-rich soil, acidic to neutral (pH 5.5 to 7), in sun or partial shade. Don't mulch the plant too heavily over winter, as the rosettes may rot.

PROPAGATION: Easy to start from seeds, which mature in autumn. Seeds need light to germinate, so sprinkle them on the soil's surface; if growing in pots, water from the bottom, so seeds aren't pushed into the soil by the force of the flow. Plants can be divided in spring or fall.

GOOD COMPANIONS: For a showstopping late-summer combination, plant cardinal flower with white turtlehead (*Chelone glabra*). Or, in one of my favorite combinations for moist, partial shade conditions, with false hellebore (*Veratrum viride*), marsh fern (*Thelypteris palustris*), boneset (*Eupatorium perfoliatum*), and great lobelia (*Lobelia siphilitica*).

RELATED SPECIES: See entry for great lobelia (*L. siphilitica*).

WILDLIFE: Attracts hummingbirds.

CHRISTMAS FERN

Polystichum acrostichoides

HEIGHT: 1–2½ feet (30–75 cm)

BLOOMING PERIOD: non-flowering

EXPOSURE: filtered light to deep shade

MOISTURE: moist to dryish

HABITAT: woodlands

RANGE: northeast

DESCRIPTION: I think of the clump-forming Christmas fern as one of our tidiest ferns, as it never looks messy or out of control. Its fronds, which range in color from light to dark green, becoming darker with age, are deeply cut – think of a comb. Evergreen and compact, leathery and glossy, its lower fronds often drape languorously on the ground (or better yet, on the snow in winter), but other fronds stay perky and upright. Don't crowd it.

MAINTENANCE AND REQUIREMENTS: This woodland fern requires rich, humusy soil with lots of organic material. It prefers moisture, but copes well with dryish conditions once established. Versatile in its light requirements, you can plant it in open to deep shade. Grows in acidic to neutral soil (pH 4.5 to 7).

PROPAGATION: Not all of the fronds are fertile and bear spores, but it's easy to identify the fertile ones as they're thinner at the top (this fertile tip withers and dies after releasing its spores). Spores appear on the underside of fronds in summer.

GOOD COMPANIONS: Such a tidy-looking fern does well with other uncomplicated – rather than blowsy or floppy – forms, I find. For example, the structural simplicity of mayapple (*Podophyllum peltatum*) looks good. If you're looking for contrast, try combining with lacier ferns, such as male fern (*Dryopteris filix-mas*), lady fern (*Athyrium filix-femina*), or maidenhair (*Adiantum pedatum*). Most plants look good against this evergreen background, but I think it's especially good as a dark foil for late-summer woodlanders that tend to turn yellowish, such as twinleaf (*Jeffersonia diphylla*) or fairy bells (*Disporum lanuginosum*), or as a contrast for berry-producing woodlanders such as white or red baneberry (*Actaea pachypoda* or *A. rubra*).

RELATED SPECIES: Braun's holly fern (*P. braunii*), a deciduous relative, is a northeastern woodland fern for cool, shaded, moist spots. See entry for sword fern (*P. munitum*) for the northwest.

COASTAL STRAWBERRY

Fragaria chiloensis

HEIGHT: 2–8 inches (5–20 cm)	**MOISTURE:** dry to moist; drought tolerant
BLOOMING PERIOD: early to late summer	**HABITAT:** meadows and dunes
EXPOSURE: sun to partial shade	**RANGE:** northwest

DESCRIPTION: Coastal strawberry is extremely useful as a groundcover; it's easy to grow and versatile and spreads quickly from runners. Leaves are dark green, shiny, leathery, and in threes. The white flower is small (3/4 inch/.75 cm) and has five petals and a yellow center. Red fruit is prolific. Try growing it on a sandy slope requiring quick cover.

MAINTENANCE AND REQUIREMENTS: Give it room to spread, but other than that, coastal strawberry requires little in the way of maintenance. Plant in sun to partial shade, dry to moist soil. Tolerates nutrient-poor sandy soil and drought.

PROPAGATION: The fastest way to propagate coastal strawberry is to cut a rooted runner (separating it from the parent plant) and transplant it with its crown at ground level. This can be done any time.

GOOD COMPANIONS: Coastal strawberry looks great with sea blush (*Plectritis congesta*) and nodding wild onion (*Allium cernuum*).

RELATED SPECIES: In the northwest, wood strawberry (*F. vesca*) is slightly taller and is useful in light shade conditions and in rock gardens; blooms in late spring or early summer, often throughout the summer, and tolerates very acidic soil. In the northeast and prairies, a great groundcover is wild strawberry (*F. virginiana*), which can be grown in open woods or meadow gardens.

WILDLIFE: Birds love the berries – as do humans (and bears).

COMPASS PLANT

Silphium laciniatum

HEIGHT: 4–8 feet (1.2–2.4 m)
BLOOMING PERIOD: mid- to late summer
EXPOSURE: full sun
MOISTURE: average to dry; drought tolerant
HABITAT: prairies
RANGE: prairies

DESCRIPTION: All the silphiums are dramatic plants – tall with abundant, long-lasting yellow flowers. Compass plant has an unusual added attraction, though: its deeply divided leaves orient themselves north-south in the bright, midday sun, in an interesting and effective adaptation to strong, drying rays. The stem is very coarse and the plant can get floppy. A good choice for clay soil.

MAINTENANCE AND REQUIREMENTS: The main thing to keep in mind when establishing young compass plants is that they should be given plenty of room and not shaded by their neighbors. Once established, they're no work at all.

PROPAGATION: Easy to start from seeds, which ripen in mid-autumn and require moist stratification, though the plant may take many years to reach blooming size. Deep roots make division difficult.

GOOD COMPANIONS: For the look of a real tallgrass prairie, plant with big bluestem (*Andropogon gerardii*) and Indian grass (*Sorghastrum nutans*) – with all these tall growers over your head, it's easy to imagine why early settlers and natives used compass plant for navigation.

RELATED SPECIES: See entry for cup plant (*S. perfoliatum*).

WILDLIFE: Butterflies feed at its nectar and birds eat the seeds.

Creeping phlox (blue) with foamflower (white)

CREEPING PHLOX

Phlox stolonifera

HEIGHT: 10–12 inches (25–30 cm)	**MOISTURE:** moist to average
BLOOMING PERIOD: spring	**HABITAT:** rich woods
EXPOSURE: partial shade to full shade	**RANGE:** northeast

DESCRIPTION: Creeping phlox is a very hardy and attractive groundcover that is quite showy when in bloom, particularly if it's planted in masses. Clusters of blue flowers carpet the ground.

MAINTENANCE AND REQUIREMENTS: Spreading by rhizomes, creeping phlox will fill a large area, in humus-rich, slightly acidic to neutral soil, partial shade to full shade, moist to average conditions.

PROPAGATION: Start from seeds, planted fresh, or divide clumps in spring or fall.

GOOD COMPANIONS: Looks fantastic with foamflower (*Tiarella cordifolia*), and Christmas fern (*Polystichum acrostichoides*).

RELATED SPECIES: Also in rich woods in the northeast, plant wild phlox (*P. divaricata*), which has striking blue flowers and grows to 20 inches (50 cm). Garden phlox (*P. paniculata*) blooms in late summer, with clusters of pink to lavender flowers. In the prairies, try prairie phlox (*P. pilosa*), which flowers in late spring and early summer, with pink to lavender clusters, and grows in dry conditions 1 to 2 feet (30 to 60 cm). In the northwest, try spreading phlox (*P. diffusa*) as a showy groundcover, with pink flowers.

Lush groundcovers such as false Solomon's seal (*Smilacina racemosa*), right, wild ginger (*Asarum canadense*), and cinnamon fern (*Osmunda cinnamomea*) carpet this northeastern woodland slope.

CULVER'S ROOT

Veronicastrum virginicum

HEIGHT: 3–5 feet (90–150 cm)	**MOISTURE:** moist to average
BLOOMING PERIOD: mid-summer	**HABITAT:** prairies, moist meadows, open woods
EXPOSURE: full sun to partial sun	**RANGE:** prairies and northeast

DESCRIPTION: Easily one of my favorite flowers, culver's root is a showy plant for prairie and meadow gardens. I'm a fan of most plants with whorled leaves (they surround the stem), but it's the flowers of culver's root that are most distinctive – dense clusters of white blooms that taper to a pointed tip. They're like spiky wands and they last for weeks.

MAINTENANCE AND REQUIREMENTS: In the wild, culver's root grows in moist areas, but it's very adaptable in the garden – fine in average moisture or even slightly dry soil, acidic to neutral. Grow culver's root in full sun or give it a try in filtered light, at the woodland edge.

PROPAGATION: Start from seeds, which ripen in fall and require light to germinate, so spread on soil surface. Or divide plants in spring or fall.

GOOD COMPANIONS: Gorgeous with ironweed (*Vernonia fasciculata*), Queen of the prairie (*Filipendula rubra*), false sunflower (*Heliopsis helianthoides*), and wild bergamot (*Monarda fistulosa*). If you've got a large area, plant culver's root with prairie dock (*Silphium terebinthinaceum*) and black-eyed Susan (*Rudbeckia hirta*). In moist areas, combine with spotted Joe-pye weed (*Eupatorium maculatum*), swamp milkweed (*Asclepias incarnata*), blue vervain (*Verbena hastata*), and wood lily (*Lilium philadelphicum*).

WILDLIFE: Attracts butterflies and bees – mine is swarmed by bees all summer.

CUP PLANT

Silphium perfoliatum

HEIGHT: 4–9 feet (1.2–2.7 m)
BLOOMING PERIOD: summer to autumn
EXPOSURE: full sun to partial sun
MOISTURE: average to dry; drought tolerant
HABITAT: meadows, prairies, woodland edges
RANGE: prairies

DESCRIPTION: No other plant in my garden gets as many comments as the cup plant; not surprising, considering that it grows to an impossible-to-ignore 9 feet (2.7 m) and dominates the backyard with thick-stemmed clumps and abundant, long-lasting yellow flowers. Everything about this plant is over the top and dramatic: its large leaves clasp the stem, creating a fascinating, water-retaining vessel that gives this plant its name; its prolific yellow blooms last well into autumn; its stem is thick and squarish; and its urge to reproduce is unstoppable – you will find young cup plants volunteering everywhere.

MAINTENANCE AND REQUIREMENTS: This plant requires nothing in the way of care. To keep your garden from turning into a cup plant plantation, you'll need to weed out volunteers, as they pop up everywhere. Tolerates clay soil and drought.

PROPAGATION: Easy to start from seed or by dividing a young offshoot from the parent plant. Deep roots make it difficult to transplant when mature. But if you have one cup plant, you'll soon have many, many more.

GOOD COMPANIONS: Because of its sturdy stem, cup plant makes a good support for other plants, such as purple coneflower (*Echinacea purpurea*). If you're looking for equally tall natives to plant with cup plant, try tall sunflower (*Helianthus giganteus*) and tall coreopsis (*Coreopsis tripteris*). I like seeing a few silphiums – cup plant, prairie dock, compass plant – together; even though their flowers are very similar, their leaves are quite dramatically different.

RELATED SPECIES: See entry for compass plant (*S. laciniatum*). A shorter, related species is rosin weed (*S. integrifolium*), which grows 2 to 6 feet (60 to 180 cm) and has yellow flowers from summer through fall. Prairie dock (*S. terebinthinaceum*) has huge elephant-ear–like leaves, yellow flowers in summer, and grows 3 to 8 feet (1 to 2.5 m) in moist to average sites.

WILDLIFE: Hummingbirds and butterflies are attracted to cup plant for nectar; birds for the seed.

CUT-LEAVED TOOTHWORT

Dentaria laciniata

HEIGHT: 8–16 inches (20–40 cm)	**EXPOSURE:** partial shade to full shade
BLOOMING PERIOD: early spring	**MOISTURE:** moist to average
	HABITAT: rich woods
	RANGE: northeast and prairies

DESCRIPTION: Spring ephemerals (plants that flower in spring, then go dormant for the summer) such as toothwort are potent tonics against the everything-on-demand ethos: gorgeous while they're around, but get used to fleeting beauty 'cause they don't last. That said, toothwort is a charming little plant: its deeply lobed and sharply toothed leaves hug the ground, and its small white or pinkish flowers serve as prolific punctuation to the leaves' dark green. But be sure to plant something else close by to fill in the gaps left when toothwort disappears for the summer.

MAINTENANCE AND REQUIREMENTS: A plant for moist rich woods, especially floodplains, toothwort simply requires good humus-rich soil and adequate moisture in partial to full shade. It spreads well under these conditions.

PROPAGATION: Sow seeds when fresh, as soon after collection as possible. Divide rhizomes, which are very close to the soil's surface, when toothwort is dormant.

GOOD COMPANIONS: Intersperse toothwort with trout lily (*Erythronium americanum*) for a speckled yellow and white combination. To fill in the post-dormancy gaps, try moisture-loving ferns such as sensitive fern (*Onoclea sensibilis*). Also looks good with Jack-in-the-pulpit (*Arisaema triphyllum*), wild ginger (*Asarum canadense*), Christmas fern (*Polystichum acrostichoides*), and purple trillium (*Trillium erectum*).

RELATED SPECIES: Also try pepperwort (*D. diphylla*), which grows 6 inches to 1 foot (15 to 30 cm) and produces small white flowers in early spring; flowers turn pink as they fade.

DEER FERN

Blechnum spicant

HEIGHT: 1–2 feet (30–60 cm)
BLOOMING PERIOD: non-
  flowering
EXPOSURE: partial sun to
  shade

MOISTURE: moist to average;
  drought tolerant in shade
HABITAT: conifer forest
RANGE: northwest

DESCRIPTION: Deer fern is a tidy, compact, utterly charming, clump-forming fern; its evergreen fronds remind me of the regular spacing in ladders. Its narrow, leathery, and pointed fronds are shiny green; the fertile fronds grow dramatically upright in the center of the clumps and are taller than the sterile fronds. Very easy to grow in rich, acidic woodland gardens, it's one of the most elegant ferns around.

MAINTENANCE AND REQUIREMENTS: Deer fern is very common in the moist, acidic conifer forests of the Pacific Northwest, but it also grows in partly sunny conditions. Give it humus-rich soil and moisture in part sun and it will be happy. Perfect as an accent plant in a mossy bed.

PROPAGATION: Easy to divide in spring or fall, or start from spores found on fertile fronds.

GOOD COMPANIONS: I like to see deer fern as a border plant along woodland paths, where its tidy delineation announces care and design amongst wilder growth. It is also stunning in a moss bed with red huckleberry (*Vaccinium parvifolium*) and salal (*Gaultheria shallon*). In a moist setting, plant with Labrador tea (*Ledum groenlandicum*), bog cranberry (*Vaccinium oxycoccos*), and lady fern (*Athyrium filix-femina*). For foliage contrast plant deer fern with wood sorrel (*Oxalis oregana*), bunchberry (*Cornus canadensis*), piggy-back plant (*Tolmiea menziesii*), and trailing yellow violet (*Viola sempervirens*).

DUTCHMAN'S BREECHES

Dicentra cucullaria

HEIGHT: 6–10 inches (15–25 cm)
BLOOMING PERIOD: early spring
EXPOSURE: partial shade to filtered light
MOISTURE: moist to average
HABITAT: rich woods
RANGE: northeast

DESCRIPTION: Dutchman's breeches is a very delicate-looking plant, but it's easy to grow. The leaves are lacy, fernlike, and much dissected, and the flowers are small, white "pantaloons" with yellow tips, dangling from an arched stem. Dutchman's breeches is a spring ephemeral plant, which means that it goes dormant in early summer.

MAINTENANCE AND REQUIREMENTS: Give the plant rich woodland soil, with plenty of organic material, and it will be happy in moist to average, neutral conditions. Because it goes dormant in early summer, you'll want to plant a "filler" plant close by.

PROPAGATION: Start from seeds, which should be sown as soon as they ripen in early summer, or separate bulblets from mature bulbs and plant them about 1 inch (2.5 cm) deep. Seeds require cold moist stratification.

GOOD COMPANIONS: Plant with trilliums (*Trillium* spp.) and Canada mayflower (*Maianthemum canadense*), or with early meadowrue (*Thalictrum dioicum*), which blooms around the same time and has dangling, drooping, greenish white flowers.

RELATED SPECIES: In the northeast, try wild bleeding heart (*D. eximia*), which has deep pink heart-shaped flowers in spring, or the spring ephemeral squirrel corn (*D. canadensis*), which has heart-shaped white or pink flowers. For the northwest, see entry for western bleeding heart (*D. formosa*).

WILDLIFE: Pollinated by bumblebees.

Starry false Solomon's seal (*Smilacina stellata*) emerges from a bed of wild ginger (*Asarum canadense*) and lady fern (*Matteucia struthiopteris*) in this northeastern woodland garden.

EVENING PRIMROSE

Oenothera biennis

HEIGHT: 1–5 feet (30–150 cm)	**MOISTURE:** dry to average; drought tolerant
BLOOMING PERIOD: summer	**HABITAT:** meadows
EXPOSURE: full sun to partial sun	**RANGE:** northeast and prairies

DESCRIPTION: Sometimes described as a coarse and common plant, the biennial evening primrose has a lot going for it, especially if you have a large sunny area with nutrient-poor, gravelly or sandy soil. Yes, it grows in "waste" places, but that doesn't mean we should ignore its many virtues – one of which is that it attracts moths. When it blooms at night, the yellow flowers seem to glow, a compelling accent in the dark. Another virtue is that its blooms are long lasting, traveling up and down the reddish stem with daily abandon.

MAINTENANCE AND REQUIREMENTS: Although it's biennial, evening primrose self-sows prodigiously, so you'll always have volunteers, which are easy to recognize by the red tinges and white mid-vein on the flat basal rosettes. Not at all fussy, the plant will grow almost anywhere in full to partial sun, in dry to regular soil.

PROPAGATION: Easy to start from seeds, which mature in late summer, or by dividing plants in spring or fall. A single plant in the garden will quickly produce many volunteer seedlings.

GOOD COMPANIONS: Looks good with blue vervain (*Verbena hastata*), ironweed (*Vernonia* spp.), and yellow coneflower (*Ratibida pinnata*).

RELATED SPECIES: Sundrops (*O. fruticosa*) is a perennial species that blooms in mid-summer, is shorter (1 to 3 feet/30 to 90 cm) and very aggressive. One of the most arresting primroses is Missouri primrose (*O. missouriensis*), which has very large (6 inches/15 cm) lemon-yellow flowers and grows close to the ground. Showy evening primrose (*O. speciosa*) has pink flowers and grows 1 to 2 feet (30 to 60 cm). In the northwest, on dry sites, try pale evening primrose (*O. pallida*), which grows to 16 inches (40 cm) with white flowers.

FALSE SOLOMON'S SEAL

Smilacina racemosa

HEIGHT: 1–3 feet (30–90 cm)
BLOOMING PERIOD: mid- to late spring
EXPOSURE: deep shade to partial sun

MOISTURE: dry to moist
HABITAT: woodlands
RANGE: across the continent

DESCRIPTION: The leaves resemble Solomon's seal, hence the name, but the flowers are different: showy clusters of creamy white blooms appear at the tip of stems in spring. Berries start out green then turn bright red in summer. When massed in the woodland garden, the plants create a dramatic show in flower and berry, and a cooling green colony in summer. In the northwest, false Solomon's seal is a great choice for the dry soil under conifer trees.

MAINTENANCE AND REQUIREMENTS: No need to fuss or worry about false Solomon's seal. Just provide humus-rich woodland soil, acidic to neutral pH, in deep shade to partial sun, and the plant will flourish, spreading obligingly and creating a dense colony.

PROPAGATION: Some gardeners report delayed flowering after dividing clumps and transplanting, but my false Solomon's seal (salvaged from a wood lot that was being developed) put on a fabulous flower show the first spring after being manhandled (plant rescues are rarely done under ideal conditions). Divide rhizomes in early spring or fall and plant 2 inches (5 cm) deep. Plant berries when fresh – don't let them dry out.

GOOD COMPANIONS: In the northwest, under conifers, try false Solomon's seal with inside-out flower (*Vancouveria hexandra*), trillium (*Trillium ovatum*), and vanilla leaf (*Achlys triphylla*). In regular soil, combine with Canada mayflower (*Maianthemum dilatatum*) and twinflower (*Linnaea borealis*). In the northeast, false Solomon's seal looks great with woodlanders such as trillium (*Trillium* spp.), blue cohosh (*Caulophyllum thalicroides*), and spikenard (*Aralia racemosa*).

RELATED SPECIES: Starry false Solomon's seal (*S. stellata*) looks very similar but has black-striped berries.

WILDLIFE: Birds eat the berries.

FALSE SUNFLOWER

Heliopsis helianthoides

HEIGHT: 3–5 feet (90–150 cm)
BLOOMING PERIOD: summer through autumn
EXPOSURE: full sun to partial sun
MOISTURE: average to dry; drought tolerant
HABITAT: prairies, meadows, woodland edge
RANGE: prairies

DESCRIPTION: The cheerful, long-lasting yellow flowers of false sunflower are lovely. The plant is very aggressive, so don't plant it if space is at a premium. A good choice for clay soil.

MAINTENANCE AND REQUIREMENTS: Like so many of the prairie natives, false sunflower could not be easier to grow; don't worry about soil amendments or watering; all it needs is full to partial sun. Deadhead the flowers and you'll have blooms from mid-summer through to fall. My false sunflower acts as an aphid trap in the garden – the bugs gravitate to the plants and leave all others alone. Every few weeks, I spray it with soapy water; some years, I ignore the aphids and just let them weaken the plant (a natural control of its aggressive tendencies).

PROPAGATION: Very easy to start from seed or by dividing clumps in spring or fall.

GOOD COMPANIONS: Because it has such a long period of bloom, you can make some interesting combinations with false sunflower. In early summer, try prairie larkspur (*Delphinium virescens*) or New Jersey tea (*Ceanothus americanus*); in mid-summer, rattlesnake master (*Eryngium yuccifolium*) or culver's root (*Veronicastrum virginicum*); in later summer, liatris (*Liatris* spp.) or any of the purply blue asters, such as sky blue aster (*Aster azureus*).

RELATED SPECIES: The true prairie sunflowers are in the *Helianthus* genus, and there are many to choose from, all with attractive yellow flowers: the annual common sunflower (*H. annuus*), which grows 5 feet (150 cm); prairie sunflower (*H. pauciflorus*), with its dark red-purple disk center; and the tallest, Maximilian sunflower (*H. maximilianii*), which grows up to 9 feet (2.7 m).

MISCELLANY: Also known as ox-eye, which gets confusing, because there's a common non-native also known as ox-eye daisy (*Chrysanthemum* x *superbum*).

FANCY WOOD FERN

Dryopteris intermedia

HEIGHT: 2–3 feet (60–90 cm)
BLOOMING PERIOD: non-flowering
EXPOSURE: deep shade to filtered light
MOISTURE: moist
HABITAT: woodlands
RANGE: northeast

DESCRIPTION: This fern is a great choice for the deeply shaded woodland garden. Its long lacy foliage is very wide (up to 10 inches/20 cm) and pointy. The shape of the whole fern is vase-like, and it is graceful and frilly. Although it does not spread quickly, it tends to stay evergreen.

MAINTENANCE AND REQUIREMENTS: Fancy wood fern requires moist, humus-rich, well-drained soil that is neutral to slightly acidic. It also does well in rocky soil, as long as it gets moisture. Mulch this fern with dead leaves to conserve moisture and replenish the soil with compost or leaf mold.

PROPAGATION: Spores mature in mid-summer. This species reputedly takes more time and care to propagate than other ferns. Be careful to ensure that the potting soil is sterile, and keep soil and germinated plants misted with water. You can also divide mature plants in spring or fall.

GOOD COMPANIONS: Fancy wood fern combines well with other shade-loving woodlanders for rich soil, such as bloodroot (*Sanguinaria canadensis*), sharp-lobed hepatica (*Hepatica acutiloba*), Jack-in-the-pulpit (*Arisaema triphyllum*), and foamflower (*Tiarella cordifolia*).

RELATED SPECIES: There are many dryopteris species from which to choose, though not all are readily available in the nursery trade – you may need to hunt (or try propagating from spores found in wild populations). Goldie's wood fern (*D. goldiana*) is the largest (to 4 feet/120 cm) and grows in moist, rich woods in the northeast, as do marginal shield fern (*D. marginalis*), which is evergreen and grows to 2 feet (60 cm), and crested shield fern (*D. cristata*), which grows to 2½ feet (75 cm) in wet woods. The most commonly available relative is male fern (*D. filix-mas*), which narrows at both the tip and base, grows to 3 feet (90 cm) and has beautiful fronds that turn from yellow-green to deep green. In the northwest, try spiny wood fern (*D. expansa*), which has broad triangular fronds and grows in full shade.

FIREWEED

Epilobium angustifolium

HEIGHT: 3–6 feet (90–180 cm)	**MOISTURE:** dry to moist
BLOOMING PERIOD: mid-summer	**HABITAT:** recently cleared woodlands, meadows
EXPOSURE: sun	**RANGE:** across the continent

DESCRIPTION: It's all a matter of perspective: the things about this plant that have been dismissed as "coarse" are precisely those features that appeal to me: its eye-popping pink color, its tall growth, its rapid spreading, and its fluffy white seedheads that cover the garden with soft down in late summer. Yes, fireweed is a colonizer – give it lots of room and give in. One interesting feature of the flower is that it begins blooming at the bottom of the stalk, then moves up.

MAINTENANCE AND REQUIREMENTS: Fireweed is an early colonizer – it's often the first plant to appear in a burned-out area, its magenta flower matching flames for brilliance. This provides an important clue about the ecology of the plant: it's tough. Egging it along isn't a problem if it's in a sunny spot, but controlling its growth may be. Plant it in a large container, or thin seedlings assiduously, if rampant growth isn't what you're after.

PROPAGATION: Chances are you won't need to worry about propagation (it does more than enough propagating without any help from gardeners), but you can easily start from seed or divide rhizomes in early spring or late fall.

GOOD COMPANIONS: Looks good with pearly everlasting (*Anaphalis margaritacea*).

WILDLIFE: Attracts bees, moths, and hummingbirds. Larval food for the white-lined sphinx moth.

MISCELLANY: Also known as willow herb, probably because of its willow-like leaves, a much more graceful name for this plant.

FLOWERING SPURGE

Euphorbia corollata

HEIGHT: 1–3 feet (30–90 cm)
BLOOMING PERIOD: summer to fall
EXPOSURE: sun to filtered light
MOISTURE: average to dry; drought tolerant
HABITAT: open woods, meadows, prairies
RANGE: prairies and northeast

DESCRIPTION: Think of the flowers you used to draw as a kid – five round petals surrounding a circle. That's flowering spurge's simple but pleasing form. It is airy and delicate-looking, its branched stems bearing a mass of flowers that bloom for long periods throughout the summer and into fall. The leaves are also appealing: bright green, long, and narrow, turning red in the fall. Flowering spurge can be aggressive.

MAINTENANCE AND REQUIREMENTS: Flowering spurge isn't the least bit fussy. You can grow it in sun to filtered light, average to dry soil conditions, sand to clay, slightly acidic to neutral soil.

PROPAGATION: Seeds mature in early fall (though they are hard to collect, because the plant expels them when ripe). Easy to divide in spring or fall, or to propagate via root cuttings.

GOOD COMPANIONS: Plant with purple coneflower (*Echinacea purpurea*), blazing star (*Liatris* spp.), showy tick trefoil (*Desmodium canadense*), Virginia mountain mint (*Pycnanthemum virginianum*), wild bergamot (*Monarda fistulosa*), and prairie dock (*Silphium terebinthinaceum*). Another lovely combination is with wild senna (*Cassia hebecarpa*), nodding onion (*Allium cernuum*), lance-leaved coreopsis (*Coreopsis lanceolata*), and prairie dropseed (*Sporobolus heterolepis*).

RELATED SPECIES: Snow-on-the-mountain (*E. marginata*) is a familiar green and white annual foliage plant for prairie gardens; attracts butterflies.

MISCELLANY: Leafy spurge (*E. esula*) is an introduced, non-native weed that is spreading invasively in the prairies.

One of the splashiest spring combinations for the northeastern woodland garden includes Virginia bluebells
(*Mertensia virginica*) and wood poppy (*Stylophorum diphyllum*).

FOAMFLOWER

Tiarella cordifolia

HEIGHT: 6–12 inches (15–30 cm)
BLOOMING PERIOD: mid-spring
EXPOSURE: full to light shade
MOISTURE: average to moist
HABITAT: rich woods
RANGE: prairies and northeast

DESCRIPTION: A dazzling groundcover when grown in masses, foamflower sends up spikes covered in small white star-like flowers in a billowy cloud in mid-spring. Flowers last for a good three weeks. The maple-like leaves – often a light green in filtered light conditions and darker green in full shade – look good throughout the summer. Foamflower is great as an edging plant, especially around woodland paths, and is also a good choice for shady rock gardens. Its shallow roots make it ideal for use around the base of trees or in areas without a deep soil layer.

MAINTENANCE AND REQUIREMENTS: Foamflower does best in rich soil, full of organic matter, acidic to neutral (pH 5 to 7), in deep to partial shade. The soil should not dry out during the growing season, so mulch with dead leaves or compost.

PROPAGATION: Foamflower's tiny seeds need light to germinate, so scatter them on top of the soil in mid-summer. Spreads by stolons; make stolon cuttings in fall to increase the colony.

GOOD COMPANIONS: The white of foamflower sets off the bright blue of wild phlox (*Phlox divaricata*) particularly well. Any of the woodland spring ephemerals, such as Virginia bluebells (*Mertensia virginica*) and trout lily (*Erythronium americanum*), are also good companions, as foamflower will cover up spaces left when the ephemerals are finished blooming. Also looks nice around the evergreen Christmas fern (*Polystichum acrostichoides*) with yellow trillium (*Trillium sessile*) and bluets (*Houstonia caerulea*).

RELATED SPECIES: The western species, *T. unifoliata* and *T. trifoliata*, grow a bit taller (16 to 20 inches/40 to 50 cm) and have more delicate blooms.

FOXGLOVE BEARDTONGUE

Penstemon digitalis

HEIGHT: 2–4 feet (60–120 cm)
BLOOMING PERIOD: early summer
EXPOSURE: sun to partial shade
MOISTURE: moist to dry
HABITAT: prairies, meadows, open woods
RANGE: prairies and northeast

DESCRIPTION: For the open woodland garden, foxglove beardtongue provides a welcome show of prolific white flowers in early summer, after the more declarative spring bloomers have peaked. It's also useful in the prairie or meadow garden, blooming before the great bulk of prairie natives begin their show. For the best effect, plant a couple of beardtongues together rather than isolating single plants here and there – you'll have a sea of white blooms in early summer.

MAINTENANCE AND REQUIREMENTS: Foxglove beardtongue is very useful in the dry shade of an open woodland garden, but it will also thrive in richer woodland soil conditions (as long as it gets some sun) and in sunny meadows and prairies. Slightly acidic to neutral soil.

PROPAGATION: Easy to start from seeds, which ripen in autumn and require cold moist stratification and light to germinate. Divide mature plants in spring or fall.

RELATED SPECIES: In the northeast and tallgrass prairie regions, other penstemons to try include hairy beardtongue (*P. hirsutus*), which has lavender trumpet-shaped flowers in early summer, and large-flowered beardtongue (*P. grandiflorus*), with lavender flowers and bluish green leaves. In the northwest, there are many penstemons from which to choose, almost all of them excellent for the garden. *P. cardwellii* produces masses of rosy purple flowers in early summer and grows to 1 foot (30 cm) in full sun and well-drained soil. *P. davidsonii*, with purple flowers, is great for the rock garden, as is shrubby penstemon (*P. fruticosus*), which has purple flowers and is drought tolerant.

WILDLIFE: Attracts hummingbirds.

GIANT HYSSOP

Agastache foeniculum

HEIGHT: 2–4 feet (60–120 cm)
BLOOMING PERIOD: summer
EXPOSURE: full sun to
partial sun
MOISTURE: dry to average;
drought tolerant
HABITAT: prairies, thickets
RANGE: prairies and northeast

DESCRIPTION: Nothing too dramatic about giant hyssop, but it is a stalwart in the garden. Lavender to violet-blue flowers are borne on a sturdy, erect spike. Leaves, which are a bit downy on the underside, give off the scent of anise, especially when bruised.

MAINTENANCE AND REQUIREMENTS: Giant hyssop is not demanding or difficult to grow. Give it average to dry soil, in full to partial sun, in loamy (but not rich) to sandy soil, and it will do just fine.

PROPAGATION: Very easy to start from seeds, which ripen in the autumn. Or divide the plant in spring or fall.

GOOD COMPANIONS: The soft lavender of giant hyssop looks good with the yellow of many prairie natives. For a drought-tolerant planting, combine with black-eyed Susan (*Rudbeckia hirta*), blazing star (*Liatris* spp.), and false sunflower (*Heliopsis helianthoides*). Also looks good with the sunflowers (*Helianthus* spp.).

RELATED SPECIES: Purple giant hyssop (*A. scrophulariaefolia*) looks very similar, but grows in wetter conditions and also in more shade, 2 to 5 feet (60 to 150 cm). Yellow giant hyssop (*A. nepetoides*) has a yellow flower spike and grows well at the edge of a woodland border, 2 to 4 feet (60 to 120 cm).

WILDLIFE: Attracts butterflies and hummingbirds.

GOLDEN ALEXANDERS

Zizia aurea

HEIGHT: 1–3 feet (30–90 cm)	**MOISTURE:** moist to dry
BLOOMING PERIOD: mid-spring to early summer	**HABITAT:** prairies, moist meadows, and moist woods
EXPOSURE: full sun to partial sun	**RANGE:** prairies and northeast

DESCRIPTION: Golden alexanders does double-duty – first, in spring, with its airy displays of small bright yellow flowers, borne in slightly domed umbels, then throughout the summer, when its dry seedheads turn a beautiful purple (other than their color, the pods look a bit like dill seed pods). Leaves are also quite attractive, a deep rich green and divided into threes.

MAINTENANCE AND REQUIREMENTS: A versatile plant, golden alexanders does well in moist to dry soil, full to partial sun, and acidic to neutral soil (pH 4 to 6.5). It spreads well on its own (indeed, can become invasive) and requires nothing in the way of special care.

PROPAGATION: Very easy to start from seeds, which ripen in late summer and require cold moist stratification, or by dividing the plant when dormant in spring.

GOOD COMPANIONS: One of the cheeriest spring plant combinations I've ever seen was golden alexanders with prairie smoke (*Geum triflorum*), the bright yellow umbels contrasting beautifully with the purple wisps of prairie smoke. In moist areas, combine with Canada anemone (*Anemone canadensis*).

RELATED SPECIES: Heart-leaved meadow parsnip (*Z. aptera*) grows best in drier prairie sites.

GOLDEN RAGWORT

Senecio aureus

HEIGHT: 1–3 feet (30–90 cm)
BLOOMING PERIOD: spring to early summer
EXPOSURE: partial shade to sun

MOISTURE: moist to average
HABITAT: moist woods, moist meadows
RANGE: northeast and prairies

DESCRIPTION: Golden ragwort is a fine addition for moist to average conditions, partially shaded sites, where it puts on a good show of long-lasting, abundant yellow flowers. At the base, leaves are heart-shaped, becoming finely cut up the stem. Golden ragwort readily self-sows.

MAINTENANCE AND REQUIREMENTS: Although golden ragwort grows in moist sites in the wild, it will do fine in average conditions in the garden, in partial shade to sun.

PROPAGATION: Propagate by seeds, which mature in late summer and require cold moist stratification, or by dividing clumps in spring or fall.

GOOD COMPANIONS: In partial shade, works well with wild phlox (*Phlox divaricata*), columbine (*Aquilegia canadensis*), and inkberry shrub (*Ilex glabra*). It can also be used as a companion for Virginia bluebells (*Mertensia virginica*) in partial shade, and it will cover the holes left when bluebells go dormant.

RELATED SPECIES: In the prairie region, try prairie ragwort (*S. plattensis*), which grows to 2 feet (60 cm), in dry, sandy, or gravelly soil and blooms in mid-spring to early summer. In the northwest, in moist open woods, try arrowleaf groundsel (*S. triangularis*), which has small yellow flowers and grows 1 to 5 feet (30 to 150 cm), or Canadian butterweed (*S. pauperculus*), also with yellow flowers, 1 to 2 feet (30 to 60 cm).

GREAT LOBELIA

Lobelia siphilitica

HEIGHT: 1–3 feet (30–90 cm)	**MOISTURE:** moist to average
BLOOMING PERIOD: late summer	**HABITAT:** woods, wet meadows
EXPOSURE: sun to partial shade	**RANGE:** prairies and northeast

DESCRIPTION: Just what we need in late summer – a dash of bright blue in the woodland garden. Great lobelia's flowers cover the thick, tall-growing spike and look particularly dramatic in clumps. In early summer, it's a pleasant enough foliage plant, with deep green leaves.

MAINTENANCE AND REQUIREMENTS: Moisture is the most important requirement of great lobelia; don't let the soil dry out. In average soil conditions, you may need to water occasionally. Other than that, it's quite versatile, growing in sun to partial shade, slightly acidic to neutral soil. Mulch to conserve moisture and replenish the soil with compost and leaf mold in the spring.

PROPAGATION: Start from seeds, which mature in fall and should be planted on the soil surface, or divide clumps in spring.

GOOD COMPANIONS: For a striking red and blue combination, grow it with cardinal flower (*Lobelia cardinalis*). In sunnier sites, grow it with flowering spurge (*Euphorbia corollata*), flat-topped aster (*Aster umbellatus*), spotted Joe-pye weed (*Eupatorium maculatum*), and white turtlehead (*Chelone glabra*). Looks best in masses, rather than single specimens.

RELATED SPECIES: See entry for cardinal flower (*L. cardinalis*).

This northeastern meadow is just two years old and already looks well established, with the wild bergamot (*Monarda fistulosa*) and black-eyed Susan (*Rudbeckia hirta*) in full bloom.

INDIAN GRASS

Sorghastrum nutans

HEIGHT: 3–8 feet (.9–2.4 m)	**MOISTURE:** average to dry; drought tolerant
BLOOMING PERIOD: late summer to fall	**HABITAT:** prairies, dry fields
EXPOSURE: full sun	**RANGE:** prairies and northeast

DESCRIPTION: A graceful, tall-growing plant, Indian grass is a signature plant of the tallgrass prairie, but it also grows farther east, into Quebec and New England. Its bright yellow flowers, which are tiny but prominent, flutter in the wind. Its seedheads are silky tassels of gold-bronze in autumn; leaves are also bronze in fall. Grow it in masses for a wild look or as a focal point in a more formal garden.

MAINTENANCE AND REQUIREMENTS: Indian grass prefers well-drained soil, from average to dry, but it also tolerates clay. It can get aggressive.

PROPAGATION: Easy to start from seeds, which ripen in late fall.

GOOD COMPANIONS: Indian grass will outcompete – both in appearance and in growth habit – any delicate plant, so plant it with other stately and tough prairie natives such as big bluestem (*Andropogon gerardii*) and tall coreopsis (*Coreopsis tripteris*). For an unusual look in a large area, why not consider an all-native grass planting? Use prairie dropseed (*Sporobolus heterolepis*) as the very ornamental edging plant (it grows in wonderfully controlled, low mounds), perhaps interplanted with June grass (*Koeleria cristata*), which grows to 2 feet (60 cm) and has large silvery green seedheads in early summer. Behind these low growers, plant little bluestem (*Andropogon scoparius*), sideoats grama (*Bouteloua curtipendula*), and mid-height prairie wildflowers such as butterfly weed (*Asclepias tuberosa*) and black-eyed Susan (*Rudbeckia hirta*). Then, for height, Indian grass, big bluestem (*A. gerardii*), and switchgrass (*Panicum virgatum*), which grows 3 to 6 feet (.9 to 1.8 m), has airy seedheads and turns golden yellow in fall. Once established, you'll never need to water this attractive grouping.

WILDLIFE: Attracts birds, which eat the seeds. Also a larval host plant for the little wood satyr butterfly and pepper and salt skipper.

INSIDE-OUT FLOWER

Vancouveria hexandra

HEIGHT: 6–20 inches (15–50 cm)	**EXPOSURE:** full shade to partial shade
BLOOMING PERIOD: spring to early summer	**MOISTURE:** moist to average
	HABITAT: coniferous woods
	RANGE: northwest

DESCRIPTION: Yes, as the name suggests, the small white flowers do look as if they are inside out, as the petals sweep backwards and flare, and the tips go outwards. Basal leaves are interesting too, like hexagons. A fine choice for a groundcover in shady woodlands.

MAINTENANCE AND REQUIREMENTS: Woodland soil, acidic to slightly neutral, in full to partial shade, will keep this plant thriving, as long as it doesn't dry out.

PROPAGATION: From seeds or by division.

GOOD COMPANIONS: Under the shade of a vine maple, plant with trillium (*Trillium ovatum*), dull Oregon grape (*Mahonia nervosa*), and vanilla leaf (*Achlys triphylla*). Also looks good with sword fern (*Polystichum munitum*), wood sorrel (*Oxalis oregana*), Siberian candyflower (*Montia sibirica*), and western bleeding heart (*Dicentra formosa*).

WILDLIFE: Attracts wasps and ants.

JACK-IN-THE-PULPIT

Arisaema triphyllum

HEIGHT: 1–3 feet (30–90 cm)	**MOISTURE:** moist to average
BLOOMING PERIOD: spring	**HABITAT:** rich woods
EXPOSURE: full to partial shade	**RANGE:** northeast

DESCRIPTION: I'm tempted to say that Jack strains my descriptive powers – just look at the photo! – especially since I'm lazy about proper botanical names for plant parts, but here goes: the green (sometimes streaked with purplish brown) spathe or hood cloaks the thick club or spadix sticking up from the center. The spathe is curled with an elegant, spadix-protecting droop. Leaves are large, on long stems. Clusters of red berries appear in late summer.

MAINTENANCE AND REQUIREMENTS: Jacks are denizens of rich moist deciduous woods and, as such, require similar conditions in the woodland garden: give them humus-rich soil, on the moist side, acidic to neutral soil (pH 5 to 6.5), in full to partial shade.

PROPAGATION: Jack-in-the-pulpit grows slowly from seed (sometimes taking two years to germinate), but if you're a patient sort, give it a try: collect ripe berries in early fall, mash them a bit, and plant fresh before they've had a chance to dry out. You can also separate cormlets, which sprout around the edges of the parent corm, in fall.

GOOD COMPANIONS: Rather than bunching them together, I prefer to see Jacks as perky accents, a few here and there. Likewise, I think they look best when rising out of a mass of some low-growing groundcover, such as violets (*Viola* spp.), wild ginger (*Asarum canadense*), or creeping phlox (*Phlox stolonifera*). Put them where you will appreciate the red berries in early autumn.

RELATED SPECIES: Green dragon (*A. dracontium*) is an arresting sight: sometimes growing 4 feet (120 cm) tall, its green spadix has a long tapering tip (the dragon's tongue).

MISCELLANY: Jack-in-the-pulpits are often dug from the wild, so buy them only from nurseries that guarantee their stock is nursery propagated.

JACOB'S LADDER

Polemonium reptans

HEIGHT: 1–1½ feet (30–45 cm)
BLOOMING PERIOD: spring to early summer
EXPOSURE: shade to filtered light
MOISTURE: moist to average
HABITAT: woods
RANGE: northeast and prairies

DESCRIPTION: The foliage alone is a good enough reason to plant Jacob's ladder: numerous paired leaflets form a kind of ladder. But the flowers are also very attractive – abundant violet-blue bells that cover the plant. Jacob's ladder spreads quickly, forming groundcovering carpets.

MAINTENANCE AND REQUIREMENTS: Jacob's ladder prefers rich soil, full of organic matter, and does well in slightly acidic to neutral conditions in filtered sun to shade. In prolonged periods of drought, it may go dormant.

PROPAGATION: Easy to start from seeds, which ripen in late summer. Plants can also be divided in early spring.

GOOD COMPANIONS: Plant with any of the woodland ferns, or for a nice contrast of foliage, plant with bloodroot (*Sanguinaria canadensis*). I particularly like to see it with small, white, delicate woodland flowers such as false rue anemone (*Isopyrum biternatum*), rue anemone (*Anemonella thalictroides*), and sharp-lobed hepatica (*Hepatica acutiloba*), or with the lemon yellow of large-flowered bellwort (*Uvularia grandiflora*).

RELATED SPECIES: In the northwest, in poor, gravelly, or sandy soil, try showy Jacob's ladder (*P. pulcherrimum*), which has blue flowers and grows to 20 inches (50 cm) in sun or shade. Two alpine species, *P. elegans* and *P. viscosum*, are both low growing with blue flowers.

LANCE-LEAVED COREOPSIS

Coreopsis lanceolata

HEIGHT: 1–2 feet (30–60 cm)	**MOISTURE:** dry to average; drought tolerant
BLOOMING PERIOD: summer	**HABITAT:** prairies and meadows
EXPOSURE: full sun	**RANGE:** prairies

DESCRIPTION: Coreopsis is one of the cheeriest plants of the sunny garden: its long-lasting yellow flowers are prolific and dependable; if you deadhead plants, you'll have blooms throughout the summer. The plant is nicely rounded in growth habit, and the leaves are narrow. A very good choice for summer bloom in a dry, sunny bed.

MAINTENANCE AND REQUIREMENTS: Its reliable blooming and drought tolerance make coreopsis a winner, particularly in sandy, nutrient-poor soils. Give it good drainage, acidic to neutral soil, full sun, and room to spread. Deadhead or cut the whole plant back in mid-summer to extend blooming.

PROPAGATION: Easy to start from seeds, which mature approximately four weeks after flowers die off; seeds do not require cold stratification. You can also divide the plant in fall or spring – a good idea not only as a propagation technique, but also to reduce overcrowding.

GOOD COMPANIONS: A lovely and striking combination is coreopsis with June grass (*Koeleria cristata*) and butterfly weed (*Asclepias tuberosa*).

RELATED SPECIES: Many species of coreopsis are available in the nursery trade: try stiff coreopsis (*C. palmata*), which grows 1 to 2 1/2 feet (30 to 75 cm) and has pale yellow flowers. The most dramatic species is tall coreopsis (*C. tripteris*), which grows on slender stalks to 8 feet (2.4 m) with yellow flowers in mid-summer through fall.

WILDLIFE: Nectar attracts butterflies and bees.

LARGE-FLOWERED BELLWORT

Uvularia grandiflora

HEIGHT: 1–2 feet (30–60 cm)
BLOOMING PERIOD: spring
EXPOSURE: deep shade to partial shade
MOISTURE: average
HABITAT: woods, thickets
RANGE: northeast

DESCRIPTION: A very interesting-looking plant, large-flowered bellwort always elicits comments in my garden. Its lemon-yellow flowers are drooping bells and a cheery sight in spring. Foliage is lighter green than many woodland plants, providing a nice contrast. Its fruit is also interesting – a small, three-cornered capsule.

MAINTENANCE AND REQUIREMENTS: Bellwort prefers rich woodland soil, neutral pH, in full to partial shade. However, I grow mine in dry woodland soil and it's doing just fine, suggesting that bellwort is more adaptable than most woodlanders. Mulch the soil with compost or leaf mold.

PROPAGATION: Easiest to divide clumps in spring or fall. Can also start from seeds, which should be sown as soon as they are ripe in late summer.

GOOD COMPANIONS: Bellwort and Virginia bluebells (*Mertensia virginica*) are easily one of the most beautiful woodland combinations there is. An added bonus: bellwort's foliage will fill in the gaps left when bluebells go dormant. Also looks good with Christmas fern (*Polystichum acrostichoides*), squirrel corn (*Dicentra canadensis*), and mayapple (*Podophyllum peltatum*).

RELATED SPECIES: A smaller but very similar species is sessile bellwort (*U. sessilifolia*), which grows 6 to 12 inches (15 to 30 cm) and prefers moist soil. Also try perfoliate bellwort (*U. perfoliata*).

MISCELLANY: Also known as merrybells. Sessile bellwort is also known as wild oats.

Wood sorrel (*Oxalis oregana*) is a subtle and attractive groundcover for northwest woodland gardens.

MAIDENHAIR FERN

Adiantum pedatum

Maidenhair fern (bottom right) with bloodroot (bottom left) and early meadowrue (middle right)

HEIGHT: 1–2 feet (30–60 cm)

BLOOMING PERIOD: non-flowering

EXPOSURE: full shade to partial shade

MOISTURE: moist

HABITAT: rich woods

RANGE: prairies and northeast

DESCRIPTION: I suspect that my affection for the maidenhair is rooted in a dubious source: it was the first fern I could identify without recourse to the field guide, so it boosted my self-esteem. But aside from that, the deciduous maidenhair is one of the most beautiful ferns. Delicate and lacy, its fronds fan out in semi-circles from purplish brown wiry stems, and once identified, you will not forget its distinctive appearance. Relatively slow to spread from creeping rhizomes, maidenhair looks best in positions of prominence, for example along the edge of a woodland path, where its unique charms can be appreciated.

MAINTENANCE AND REQUIREMENTS: A fern of the woods, maidenhair prefers a sheltered spot in medium shade but will also do well in deep shade. Soil should be rich, full of organic matter, and moist – if it dries out, the fronds become crispy. Mulch it to conserve moisture.

PROPAGATION: Spores mature in late summer and fall. Tap spores into sterile potting mix; mist with water; cover with clear plastic lid to keep moist. Mature plants can be divided in early spring or late fall.

GOOD COMPANIONS: In the northeast, maidenhair looks good with many other woodland ferns, especially goldie's wood fern (*Dryopteris goldiana*). I also like to see it surrounded by low-growing groundcovers, such as wild ginger (*Asarum canadense*), the fern rising above the woodland carpet. A larger woodlander that holds its own in visual competition with maidenhair is black snakeroot (*Cimicifuga racemosa*).

RELATED SPECIES: The western maidenhair fern (*A. aleuticum*) has a very similar appearance and requirements. Many nurseries in the northwest sell the prairie and northeastern maidenhair fern as a native, but it is a different species.

MAYAPPLE

Podophyllum peltatum

HEIGHT: 1½ feet (45 cm)
BLOOMING PERIOD: late spring
EXPOSURE: deep shade to filtered sun

MOISTURE: moist to average
HABITAT: woodlands and openings
RANGE: northeast and prairies

DESCRIPTION: Parasol is too dainty a word; instead, think squadron of burly soldiers, all lined up with closed umbrellas. As the leaves open, rising upwards until parallel with the ground, the mayapple colony becomes a hovering mass of deeply lobed dark green foliage, each leaf as wide as 1 foot (30 cm). Hidden underneath the leaves, in the crotch of the stem, a single white flower appears in late spring. Later in the summer, a large, pale yellow berry appears.

MAINTENANCE AND REQUIREMENTS: Mayapple does best in rich, woodsy, neutral to slightly acidic soil, spreading rapidly by underground rhizomes, producing a dense colony. Give it plenty of room and use a mulch to conserve moisture. During prolonged periods of drought it may go dormant, but don't worry, it will return next year. Grows in deep shade to filtered sunlight.

PROPAGATION: The easiest way to propagate mayapple (other than to just leave it alone to spread on its own steam, that is) is by root division in the fall. Plant root divisions about 1 inch (2.5 cm) deep. Seeds require cold moist stratification.

GOOD COMPANIONS: Mayapple looks best in masses, rather than interplanted with other species (besides, it will probably outcompete any companions). However, plant another vigorous grower, such as wild ginger (*Asarum canadense*), along the edges of the colony if you want to control mayapple's spread. Mayapple works well as a filler for the holes left by spring ephemerals such as trout lily (*Erythronium americanum*).

MISCELLANY: Mayapple berries are toxic when young, but edible when ripe. Some people make mayapple jelly.

MICHIGAN LILY

Lilium michiganense

HEIGHT: 3–6 feet (90–180 cm)
BLOOMING PERIOD: summer
EXPOSURE: full sun to partial sun
MOISTURE: moist
HABITAT: moist meadows, open woods
RANGE: prairies and northeast

DESCRIPTION: All of the native lilies are showy, dramatic plants for the garden. Michigan lily grows very tall – on a stem that may need staking – and has lovely deep orange flowers, dotted with brown, and petals that curve backwards.

MAINTENANCE AND REQUIREMENTS: Michigan lily requires moist soil. It will do well in sun to partial sun and it prefers rich, fertile, neutral soil. Dig in lots of compost prior to planting and mulch to conserve moisture.

PROPAGATION: Start from seeds, which should be planted fresh and may take many years to reach flowering size. Or divide small bulbs from the rhizomes in fall.

GOOD COMPANIONS: In a moist bed, in partial sun, plant with tall meadowrue (*Thalictrum polygamum*), jewelweed (*Impatiens capensis*), and culver's root (*Veronicastrum virginicum*).

RELATED SPECIES: In the northeast and prairies, try turk's-cap lily (*L. superbum*), which has spotted, reddish flowers and grows 3 to 7 feet (.9 to 2 m) in moist conditions, or Canada lily (*L. canadense*), which has nodding orange, yellow, or red blooms and grows to 5 feet (1.5 m). The lovely wood lily (*L. philadelphicum*) has perky, upward-facing blooms (not the nodding or recurved shape of the other lilies) and is a brilliant orange, with spots; grows 1 to 3 feet (30 to 90 cm) in meadows and open woods. In the northwest, grow tiger lily (*L. columbianum*) in full sun to partial shade – gorgeous nodding orange flowers dotted with purplish brown; grows 1 to 3 feet (30 to 120 cm) in moist soil.

NEW ENGLAND ASTER

Aster novae-angliae

HEIGHT: 3–6 feet (.9–1.8 m)
BLOOMING PERIOD: late summer to fall
EXPOSURE: full sun to partial sun
MOISTURE: moist to dry
HABITAT: fields, meadows, moist prairies
RANGE: prairies and northeast

DESCRIPTION: The asters have been much fiddled with and hybridized by the nursery trade, but to my mind the native species are still the most attractive. New England aster is an adaptable tall grower in sunny, moist conditions. In drier, shadier sites, it doesn't get as tall and its blooms are less abundant, but it still looks good. In late summer, New England aster is covered with long-lasting purple flowers with yellow centers – a stunning sight.

MAINTENANCE AND REQUIREMENTS: In the wild, New England aster grows in moist, sunny meadows, but in the garden it's happy in average soil, acidic to neutral, and will even grow in dry or clayey conditions. If you want a more controlled, bushier plant, cut it back in mid-summer before it blooms. May have mildew problems if the plant is crowded and not getting enough air circulation, in which case, divide the plant.

PROPAGATION: Easy to start from seeds, which mature in late fall, or by dividing the plant in spring. If you have one plant, you'll soon have volunteer seedlings throughout the garden.

GOOD COMPANIONS: There's no more typical late-summer and fall combination for the prairies and northeastern meadow than New England aster and goldenrod (*Solidago* spp.). Also looks good with tall sunflower (*Helianthus giganteus*) and sneezeweed (*Helenium autumnale*).

RELATED SPECIES: In the northeast and prairies, white aster species to try include panicled aster (*A. simplex*), flat-topped aster (*A. umbellatus*), calico aster (*A. lateriflorus*), and heath aster (*A. ericoides*). Blue species include azure aster (*A. azureus*), New York aster (*A. novae-belgii*), and smooth aster (*A. laevis*). In the northwest, try showy aster (*A. conspicuus*), leafy aster (*A. foliaceus*), and great northern aster (*A. modestus*).

WILDLIFE: Attracts bees and butterflies. Asters are larval host plants for many of the crescent and checkerspot butterflies.

In the northeast and prairies, meadow gardens offer a colorful and low-maintenance alternative to lawns. Here, the spikes of blue vervain (*Verbena hastata*) combine with black-eyed Susan (*Rudbeckia hirta*), Virginia mountain mint (*Pycnanthemum virginianum*), and purple coneflower (*Echinacea purpurea*).

NEW YORK FERN

Thelypteris noveboracensis

HEIGHT: 1–2 feet (30–60 cm)	**MOISTURE:** average to moist
BLOOMING PERIOD: non-flowering	**HABITAT:** damp woods
EXPOSURE: filtered light to shade	**RANGE:** northeast

DESCRIPTION: New York fern's aggressive nature can be used to good advantage in the large woodland garden. Its elegant fronds are a rich green and taper at both the tip and the base. New York fern sends up fronds every which way from its creeping rhizome, creating dense patches of pleasing patterns. A deciduous fern, it's one of the first to turn straw-colored, and then brown, in early fall.

MAINTENANCE AND REQUIREMENTS: New York fern prefers moist, humus-rich woodland soil. Add lots of organic matter to the soil before planting and continue to supplement with compost – new fronds, creeping from the rhizomes, will appear in the rich additions of compost. Will grow in filtered light to shade; soil should be well-drained, acidic to neutral. I grow mine in dry woodland soil and while it doesn't spread, it stays healthy.

PROPAGATION: Divide rhizomes in early spring or fall. Spores mature in mid- to late summer; fertile fronds are easy to recognize as they're longer and narrower than the others.

GOOD COMPANIONS: New York fern is a great fern to use to fill in the holes left by spring ephemerals such as spring beauty (*Claytonia virginica*) and Dutchman's breeches (*Dicentra cucullaria*). It also looks good with wild phlox (*Phlox divaricata*), foamflower (*Tiarella cordifolia*), early meadowrue (*Thalictrum dioicum*), and mitrewort (*Mitella diphylla*).

RELATED SPECIES: Marsh fern (*T. palustris*) is a good choice for marshy or wet meadow sites in the northeast; spreads rapidly. Broad beech fern (*T. hexagonoptera*), which grows to 2 feet (60 cm), is useful at filling in the holes left by spring ephemerals. In the northwest, try northern beech fern (*T. phegopteris*), which is very easy to grow and reaches approximately 1 foot (30 cm) in rich woodland gardens.

NEW YORK IRONWEED

Vernonia noveboracensis

HEIGHT: 3–6 feet (90–180 cm)
BLOOMING PERIOD: mid- to late summer
EXPOSURE: sun
MOISTURE: moist to average
HABITAT: moist meadows
RANGE: prairies and northeast

DESCRIPTION: I'm a proselytizing bore on the subject of ironweed: I think every sunny garden in the northeast and prairies needs some, and I can't understand why it hasn't made the leap from field to garden more often. Maybe it's the name? Whatever the reason, ironweed is a stunner. Clusters of purplish blue to fuchsia flowers cover and crowd the top of the plant and last for weeks. Even when the flowers have dried out to a tawny gold, they're attractive. Stems are sturdy, ensuring that the plant doesn't flop over, despite its great height.

MAINTENANCE AND REQUIREMENTS: Though it grows in the wild in damp places, ironweed also flourishes in regular soil (and in my never-watered backyard, it even thrives in dry soil). Give it plenty of room. Tolerates clay and acidic to neutral conditions.

PROPAGATION: Seeds are prolific. Sow seeds thickly in late autumn. Divide in spring, or take stem cuttings in mid-summer.

GOOD COMPANIONS: To bring out the flashy brilliance even more, plant with culver's root (*Veronicastrum virginicum*) and boneset (*Eupatorium perfoliatum*). A fantastic combination, for the back of the border, is ironweed, spotted Joe-pye weed (*Eupatorium maculatum*), and sneezeweed (*Helenium autumnale*).

RELATED SPECIES: Tall ironweed (*V. altissima*) grows to 7 feet (2.1 m) or more, often flowers later, and doesn't create as bushy a plant. Western ironweed (*V. fasciculata*) has smaller, denser flower clusters and grows to 6 feet (1.8 m).

WILDLIFE: Butterflies feed on its nectar. Western ironweed is a larval host plant for the American painted lady.

NODDING WILD ONION

Allium cernuum

HEIGHT: 1–2 feet (30–60 cm)	**MOISTURE:** moist to dry; drought tolerant
BLOOMING PERIOD: mid-summer	**HABITAT:** prairies, meadows, open woods
EXPOSURE: full sun to partial sun	**RANGE:** northwest, prairies, northeast

DESCRIPTION: Nodding wild onion is a particular favorite of mine, at all of its stages. Its grass-like ribbony leaves are long and graceful; its flower cluster hangs down, covered with a fine onion-skin-like sheath before opening; the blooms, in mid-summer, are whitish rose-colored and bell-shaped; and its seedheads are round. Planted in groups around the edges of flower beds, it's a charmer.

MAINTENANCE AND REQUIREMENTS: Nodding wild onion grows in a wide range of conditions, from sun to partial sun, moist to dry soil, acidic to neutral, rocky to rich. Prefers good drainage, so mix some sand into heavy soil.

PROPAGATION: Easy to start from seeds, which mature in early fall and require cold moist stratification, or by dividing offset bulbs, which form beside mature bulbs, in fall or spring.

GOOD COMPANIONS: Combine with leadplant (*Amorpha canescens*), a prairie native that has purple to blue flowers in summer, and prairie dropseed (*Sporobolus heterolepis*), a wonderfully ornamental low-growing native grass.

RELATED SPECIES: In the northeast, wild leek (*A. tricoccum*) is a gorgeous woodland relative of the nodding wild onion. It grows in shady, rich conditions; its aromatic (oniony) leaves appear in early spring, then completely die back before its creamy white flowers, in a round umbel, appear. Great for early summer color in the woodland garden. Prairie onion (*A. stellatum*) is similar to nodding onion, growing in dry prairies, but its flower heads don't droop and are dark pink to lavender. In the northwest, try Hooker's onion (*A. acuminatum*), which blooms in early summer with pinkish purple flowers; grows to approximately 1 foot (30 cm).

MISCELLANY: Bulbs are edible. Chicago got its name from the Algonquin Indian name for this plant, *chigagou*.

OBEDIENT PLANT

Physostegia virginiana

HEIGHT: 1–4 feet (30–120 cm)	**MOISTURE:** moist to dry
BLOOMING PERIOD: late summer	**HABITAT:** damp thickets, prairies, and meadows
EXPOSURE: full sun to partial sun	**RANGE:** prairies and northeast

DESCRIPTION: Very showy, obedient plant has become popular in the nursery trade, even for those not growing many natives. It's easy to see why it's held in such esteem: the pink snapdragon-like flowers are borne on a spike at the top of the square stem (a mint family feature) and they last for a few weeks. There's something very *precise* about this plant. About the name: if you bend the flowers horizontally, they stay put for a while – altogether an obliging wildflower.

MAINTENANCE AND REQUIREMENTS: Obedient plant will grow in a wide range of conditions, from moist to average soil, slightly acidic to neutral, full sun to partial sun. It spreads well, creating a bushy clump.

PROPAGATION: Easy to start from seeds, which ripen in late fall, or by dividing stolons (below-ground stems) in early spring or late fall.

GOOD COMPANIONS: Looks great with sweet black-eyed Susan (*Rudbeckia subtomentosa*), purple coneflower (*Echinacea purpurea*), flowering spurge (*Euphorbia corollata*), stiff goldenrod (*Solidago rigida*), and flat-topped aster (*Aster umbellatus*).

WILDLIFE: Attracts hummingbirds.

MISCELLANY: Also known as false dragonhead.

OREGON IRIS

Iris tenax

HEIGHT: 12–16 inches (30–40 cm)	**MOISTURE:** dry to average
	HABITAT: fields, meadows, open woods
BLOOMING PERIOD: spring	
EXPOSURE: sun to open shade	**RANGE:** northwest

DESCRIPTION: Don't worry if you see this plant listed as "tough-leaved iris" in some catalogues or books (*tenax* is Latin for "tenacious"); there's nothing coarse about this plant. With large lavender to purple flowers, splashed with yellow, and dark veins, it's a showy charmer. It grows in clumps.

MAINTENANCE AND REQUIREMENTS: Oregon iris is perfect for the rock garden, as it prefers well-drained soil, in full sun to open shade. It will do well in richer soil, but doesn't require it. Oregon iris is easy to grow and although it does not spread quickly, it will form large clumps.

PROPAGATION: Start from seeds, which ripen in late summer, or by rhizome division in fall.

GOOD COMPANIONS: For a lovely blue and yellow combination, plant with cinquefoil (*Potentilla gracilis*).

RELATED SPECIES: In wet areas of the northwest, try wild flag (*I. setosa*), also with blue flowers to 18 inches (45 cm), or western blue iris (*I. missouriensis*). In the prairies and northeast, try blue flag (*I. versicolor*), which requires moist, well-drained soil in sun to part sun, and grows 1 1/2 to 2 1/2 feet (45 to 75 cm).

Northwestern woodland species such as trillium (*Trillium ovatum*), sword fern (*Polystichum munitum*), and western bleeding heart (*Dicentra formosa*) thrive in dense shade and rich soil.

OREGON SUNSHINE

Eriophyllum lanatum

HEIGHT: 1–2 feet (30–60 cm)	**HABITAT:** meadows, rocky slopes
BLOOMING PERIOD: summer	
EXPOSURE: full sun	**RANGE:** northwest
MOISTURE: dry; drought tolerant	

DESCRIPTION: A massed planting of Oregon sunshine is a bright sight in summer, when its yellow daisylike flowers are in long-lasting bloom. Deadhead and you may get a second flowering in early autumn. The leaves are also attractive: narrowly lobed, bluish gray and woolly; stems and leaves are hairy.

MAINTENANCE AND REQUIREMENTS: On dry, exposed sites, Oregon sunshine is a good choice. Soil should be well-drained, but it's fine if the soil layer is thin. Needs full sun.

PROPAGATION: Easy to start from seed or by dividing clumps in spring or fall.

GOOD COMPANIONS: Good companions include lupine – the low-growing riverbank lupine (*Lupinus rivularis*) or the taller growing large-leaved lupine (*L. polyphyllus*) – nodding wild onion (*Allium cernuum*), and sea blush (*Plectritis congesta*). Native grasses to plant with Oregon sunshine for a meadow effect include red fescue (*Festuca rubra*), blue wild rye (*Elymus glaucus*), and Idaho fescue (*F. idahoensis*).

MISCELLANY: Also known as wooly sunflower and golden yarrow. The wooly hairs help prevent evaporation from the leaves, giving this plant its drought-tolerant nature.

PASQUE FLOWER

Anemone patens

HEIGHT: 8–12 inches
(20–30 cm)
BLOOMING PERIOD: late
spring to summer
EXPOSURE: sun to partial
shade

MOISTURE: average to dry
HABITAT: prairies and meadows
RANGE: northwest, Rocky
Mountains, and prairies

DESCRIPTION: One of the most interesting features of pasque flower is that its bloom is quite large ($1^{1}/_{2}$ to 2 inches/3.8 to 5 cm) in relation to the overall size of the plant. That, in addition to the outstanding lavender color of the flowers and the general hairy look of the plant, make it a wonderful addition to the garden. Its foliage is very deeply cut, looking a bit like buttercups (*Ranunculus*).

MAINTENANCE AND REQUIREMENTS: Good drainage is important, but other than that, pasque flower is not fussy. It can be grown in sun to partial shade, dry to average conditions, neutral pH. It may go dormant during drought.

PROPAGATION: Easy to start from seeds, which appear as wispy white plumes in summer. Seeds do not require cold stratification. Pasque flower can also be propagated by division or root cuttings in early spring or late fall.

GOOD COMPANIONS: For a lavender and white combination in the northwest, plant with western pasque flower (*A. occidentalis*). In the prairies, plant with golden alexanders (*Zizea aurea*) and hairy puccoon (*Lithospermum croceum*).

RELATED SPECIES: Western pasque flower (*A. occidentalis*) is equally charming, with white flowers. Blue anemone (*A. oregana*) and western wood anemone (*A. lyallii*), which is white, are good choices for woodland conditions.

MISCELLANY: Also known as pulsatilla.

POLYPODY FERN

Polypodium virginianum

HEIGHT: 8 inches (20 cm)	**MOISTURE:** moist to dry
BLOOMING PERIOD: non-flowering	**HABITAT:** woods
EXPOSURE: open shade to deep shade	**RANGE:** prairies and northeast

DESCRIPTION: Unlike ferns such as cinnamon fern (*Osmunda cinnamomea*), which grow in vase-like clumps, polypody is a creeping fern that creates dense mats, often covering mossy rocks in the wild, seemingly growing out of almost no soil. Small, leathery, and evergreen, its frond shape is compellingly simple. Perfect for the rock garden in filtered light and open shade, though it's also tolerant of deeper shade; let it spread as a groundcover.

MAINTENANCE AND REQUIREMENTS: As is to be expected from polypody's habit of clambering over rocks, it doesn't like to soak in moisture and, thus, good drainage is important. (Moist soil is fine as long as it's well drained; also tolerant of dry soil.) Protect it from direct sun and wind. Grows in acidic to neutral soil.

PROPAGATION: Polypody spreads into dense mats via creeping roots, which can be divided in spring or fall.

GOOD COMPANIONS: Polypody is a good choice for the acid soil beneath pines or rhododendrons. Looks great with goldthread (*Coptis groenlandica*), Canada mayflower (*Maianthemum canadense*), gaywings (*Polygala paucifolia*), and bunchberry (*Cornus canadensis*).

RELATED SPECIES: In the northwest, try licorice fern (*P. glycyrrhiza*) on wet, mossy ground in shade or to cover a rotting stump. It may go dormant in hot, dry summers. Western polypody (*P. hesperium*), somewhat smaller than licorice fern, grows on rocks and cliffs.

PURPLE CONEFLOWER

Echinacea purpurea

HEIGHT: 2–5 feet (60–150 cm)	**MOISTURE:** average to dry; drought tolerant
BLOOMING PERIOD: summer to fall	**HABITAT:** prairies and open clearings
EXPOSURE: full sun to partial sun	**RANGE:** prairies

DESCRIPTION: Of all the native plants that have gained currency in the commercial nursery trade, none has been as popular as purple coneflower. Little wonder – it's a dependable, low-maintenance showy plant with a long blooming season and no pest problems. Each flower goes through an attractive and lengthy transformation: starting out pale pink and with thin, downturned petals (ray flowers), then gradually turning a deeper purple, getting bigger and the center cone becoming more pronounced and burnished-copper-colored. If you deadhead spent blooms, you will have flowers from early summer through to autumn.

MAINTENANCE AND REQUIREMENTS: Couldn't be easier. Purple coneflower is quite versatile, growing in clay to sandy soil, full to partial sun, acidic to neutral (pH 4.5 to 7.5), average to dry conditions. Deadhead to prolong blooming.

PROPAGATION: Very easy to start from seed, which ripen in late summer to fall and require cold moist stratification. If you have one purple coneflower plant, you're sure to get many volunteer seedlings quickly. It's also very easy to divide plants in spring or fall.

GOOD COMPANIONS: A classic (and zero maintenance) combination is purple coneflower with black-eyed Susan (*Rudbeckia hirta*), goldenrod (*Solidago* spp.), and yellow coneflower (*Ratibida pinnata*).

RELATED SPECIES: Pale purple coneflower (*E. pallida*) is a more elegant, less declarative species and perfect for the sunny garden. Growing 3 feet (90 cm) tall, its petal-like ray flowers are narrower than purple coneflower and a bit longer in their droop.

WILDLIFE: Great nectar plant for butterflies and hummingbirds. Small birds eat the seeds.

PURPLE PRAIRIE CLOVER

Petalostemum purpureum

HEIGHT: 1–2 feet (30–60 cm)	**MOISTURE:** average to dry; drought tolerant
BLOOMING PERIOD: early to mid-summer	**HABITAT:** dry prairies
EXPOSURE: full sun	**RANGE:** prairies

DESCRIPTION: Brilliant purple "thimbles" at the end of each stem are quite attractive – flowering progresses in a ring from the bottom up. Along with its beauty, purple prairie clover does good work in the soil-building department, as it's a nitrogen-fixing legume. Leaves are narrow, and the plant spreads well but never gets out of control.

MAINTENANCE AND REQUIREMENTS: Purple prairie clover is very dependable and requires nothing in the way of special care, other than a winter mulch for young seedlings during their first winter. Its roots penetrate very deep into the soil (at least 5 feet/1.5 m), so plant it where you won't need to move it.

PROPAGATION: Division can be tricky, because of deep roots, so start from seeds, which mature in late summer. Rub seed coats with sandpaper.

GOOD COMPANIONS: I think purple prairie clover looks especially great when combined with white flowers, such as white prairie clover (*P. candidum*), whorled milkweed (*Asclepias verticillata*), Virginia mountain mint (*Pycnanthemum virginianum*), nodding wild onion (*Allium cernuum*), and culver's root (*Veronicastrum virginicum*).

RELATED SPECIES: White prairie clover (*P. candidum*) looks very similar but has white flowers.

WILDLIFE: Attracts bees. Larval host plant for sulphur butterflies.

QUEEN OF THE PRAIRIE

Filipendula rubra

HEIGHT: 4–6 feet (1.2–1.8 m)
BLOOMING PERIOD: mid-summer
EXPOSURE: full sun
MOISTURE: moist to average
HABITAT: moist prairies, moist meadows
RANGE: prairies

DESCRIPTION: Queen of the prairie earns its name with regal carriage (tall height) and flashy but understated (a royal contradiction indeed) blooms. Billowy pink clusters of fragrant flowers grace the top of tall stems in mid-summer and last for a few weeks. Even when they turn a light brown as they dry up, they're attractive. The leaves, too, are interesting: large and each one divided into several narrow, toothed segments.

MAINTENANCE AND REQUIREMENTS: Though native to moist prairies, this plant does well in average and even dry soil conditions (mine has never been watered, except by the rain). Its tall stems sometimes get floppy, so you may need to support it with stakes.

PROPAGATION: Seeds mature approximately four to six weeks after the flowers fade; plant fresh in late summer; requires cold moist stratification. Queen of the prairie is easy to propagate by division; keep transplants well watered.

GOOD COMPANIONS: Plant with other moisture-loving tall species such as spotted Joe-pye weed (*Eupatorium maculatum*), boneset (*Eupatorium perfoliatum*), and New York ironweed (*Vernonia noveboracensis*) for a very nice combination of pink, purple and white. Also looks great with blue flag (*Iris versicolor*).

WILDLIFE: Attracts butterflies.

A prairie planting of swamp milkweed (*Asclepias incarnata*), black-eyed Susan (*Rudbeckia hirta*), liatris (*Liatris pycnostachya*), false sunflower (*Heliopsis helianthoides*), and purple coneflower (*Echinacea purpurea*) will attract butterflies all summer.

RATTLESNAKE MASTER

Eryngium yuccifolium

HEIGHT: 1–4 feet (30–120 cm)
BLOOMING PERIOD: mid-summer
EXPOSURE: full sun
MOISTURE: dry to moist; drought tolerant
HABITAT: prairies, meadows
RANGE: prairies

DESCRIPTION: This is one weird-looking plant (and I mean that as high praise). Its leaves are more like some southern desert denizen – indeed, like the yucca, hence the name – all spiky at the edges, thick and glaucous (another bias of mine – I love leaves with a bluish tinge). Its flowers are stiff-looking, whitish blue little balls at the tip of flowering stems – very 1950s (you can imagine them as a pattern on plastic dishware or linoleum floors). Such irreverence aside, rattlesnake master clearly makes a very interesting addition to the prairie garden; even after its flowers have stopped blooming, the balls remain as a pretty feature.

MAINTENANCE AND REQUIREMENTS: Rattlesnake master is a very drought-tolerant, tough plant. It thrives in dry, nutrient-poor soil, demanding nothing in the way of care. But it does require sun. Tolerates clay soil, and slightly acidic to neutral conditions.

PROPAGATION: Easy to start from seeds, which mature in fall and require cold moist stratification. Plants can also be divided, though they resent disturbance.

GOOD COMPANIONS: For a dramatic contrast of flower form and color, plant with culver's root (*Veronicastrum virginicum*), blazing star (*Liatris* spp.), and black-eyed Susan (*Rudbeckia hirta*). Also looks great with wild bergamot (*Monarda fistulosa*), yellow coneflower (*Ratibida pinnata*), and prairie dock (*Silphium terebinthinaceum*).

WILDLIFE: Nectar attracts butterflies and bees.

RED BANEBERRY

Actaea rubra

HEIGHT: 1–2 feet (30–60 cm)	**MOISTURE:** moist to average
BLOOMING PERIOD: spring	**HABITAT:** woodlands, thickets
EXPOSURE: full shade to partial shade	**RANGE:** northwest, prairies, and northeast

DESCRIPTION: Red baneberry is an excellent choice for a very shady spot. The plant gets quite bushy (almost like a shrub) and in spring, a large cluster of white flowers appears – looking like a snowball, though sometimes more oblong. In mid- to late summer, this plant has high value as an ornamental again, when its clusters of shiny red berries provide a bright accent.

MAINTENANCE AND REQUIREMENTS: Red baneberry needs rich woodland soil, full of organic matter, slightly acidic to neutral (pH 5 to 7). Give it full to partial shade and don't let the soil dry out, though average moisture conditions are fine.

PROPAGATION: Can be started from seeds, which should be planted fresh, as soon as they ripen in summer.

GOOD COMPANIONS: In the northeast, plant with white baneberry (*A. pachypoda*) for a great contrast when the berries appear. Also works well with sensitive fern (*Onoclea sensibilis*), wild ginger (*Asarum canadense*), sharp-lobed hepatica (*Hepatica acutiloba*), twinleaf (*Jeffersonia diphylla*), and violets (*Viola* spp.). In the northwest, plant with sword fern (*Polystichum munitum*).

RELATED SPECIES: White baneberry (*A. pachypoda*) looks very similar in leaf and flower, but has white berries with a red stalk and black "eye." (Also known as "doll's eyes" because of the berries.)

ROUGH BLAZING STAR

Liatris aspera

HEIGHT: 2–4 feet (60–120 cm)
BLOOMING PERIOD: mid- to late summer
EXPOSURE: full sun
MOISTURE: dry to average; drought tolerant
HABITAT: prairies, savannas, meadows
RANGE: prairies

DESCRIPTION: With good reason, all the blazing stars (also known as gayfeathers) are popular plants for prairie and meadow gardens and hence are readily available in the nursery trade. Their slender, erect spikes, covered in deep pink to purple flowers, make them a dramatic, unusual addition to the bed. Rough blazing star looks "knobblier" than many other gayfeathers, its flower heads rounder and wider spaced. Even when it's finished blooming, its spiky wands are attractive accents.

MAINTENANCE AND REQUIREMENTS: Like most prairie natives, rough blazing star requires little in the way of maintenance, thriving in dry soil and full sun, in acidic to neutral soil. If it's shaded by other plants, its stalk may become twisted rather than starkly vertical in its search for sun.

PROPAGATION: Easy to start from seeds, which mature in late fall and require cold moist stratification, or by dividing corms in early spring.

GOOD COMPANIONS: Looks great with any of the prairie and meadow species.

RELATED SPECIES: Dotted blazing star (*L. punctata*) has denser flowers and tiny narrow leaves that stick out along the flower spike. Meadow blazing star (*L. ligulistylis*) has round flowers up the spike, openly spaced like little pompoms. In the northeast, try *L. cylindracea*, which grows 8 to 18 inches (20 to 45 cm). Prairie blazing star (*L. pycnostachya*) is one of the showiest blazing stars, with narrow leaves and very dense flowers, growing in wet to average soil, clay to loam.

WILDLIFE: Attracts butterflies, hummingbirds, and bees.

SALAL

Gaultheria shallon

HEIGHT: 3–6 feet (1–2 m)
BLOOMING PERIOD: spring and summer
EXPOSURE: shade to sun
MOISTURE: dry to moist; drought tolerant once established
HABITAT: coniferous forest
RANGE: northwest

DESCRIPTION: This evergreen shrub is very useful as a groundcover, particularly in acidic, nutrient-poor sites. Its glossy, leathery leaves brighten up a dark corner; small pinkish white urn-shaped flowers appear in spring and last well; it produces edible purple berries in summer. Its reddish brown twigs are also attractive. A classic northwest scene is a nurse log covered with salal and evergreen huckleberry (*Vaccinium ovatum*).

MAINTENANCE AND REQUIREMENTS: Salal is a tough, hardy plant; it can become invasive (in the wild, it creates dense thickets). Prefers acidic soil and requires good drainage.

PROPAGATION: Start from seed, collected in late summer or fall, or take stem cuttings in fall. Can also propagate by "layering" stems (bend a branch to the ground, cover with soil, and hold down with wire), which can be cut once the layered branch has rooted in the ground.

GOOD COMPANIONS: Salal, dull Oregon grape (*Mahonia nervosa*), and sword fern (*Polystichum munitum*) – a signature combination for the northwest. Salal is a good drought-tolerant plant for the base of madrone (*Arbutus menziesii*) or big-leaf maple (*Acer macrophyllum*). Interesting woodland companions include inside-out flower (*Vancouveria hexandra*), false Solomon's seal (*Smilacina racemosa*), and small-flowered alumroot (*Heuchera micrantha*).

RELATED SPECIES: Checkerberry wintergreen (*Gaultheria procumbens*) is a good creeping evergreen, with dark leaves that turn red in fall. Has white flowers and red berries.

WILDLIFE: Birds (and humans) eat the berries. Hummingbirds feed at flowers. Larval food plant for the brown elfin butterfly.

SATIN FLOWER

Sisyrinchium douglasii

HEIGHT: 6–12 inches (15–30 cm)
BLOOMING PERIOD: early spring
EXPOSURE: full sun to open woods
MOISTURE: spring moisture but summer-drought tolerant
HABITAT: meadows, rocky bluffs, open woodlands
RANGE: northwest

DESCRIPTION: The iridescent magenta purple of satin flower is an enchanting spring sight. Although the blooms last for only a few days, they're definitely worth the short splash. The leaves are long and thin, almost like a stout grass or iris leaf.

MAINTENANCE AND REQUIREMENTS: Satin flower requires moderately rich soil and moisture in spring.

PROPAGATION: Divide or start from seed (though germination is reported to be low).

GOOD COMPANIONS: Looks great with camas (*Camassia quamash*), stonecrop (*Sedum spathulifolium*), white fawn lily (*Erythronium oregonum*), and broad-leaved shooting star (*Dodecatheon hendersonii*).

RELATED SPECIES: In moist areas of the northwest, try golden-eyed grass (*S. californicum*), which has yellow flowers with dark veins and opens only in the morning, closing up at midday; it prefers moist areas in partial shade to full sun. In central Canada, the midwest, and into the northeast and Great Lakes, try *S. angustifolium*, which has violet to blue flowers in late spring and early summer. In the prairies, try prairie blue-eyed grass (*S. campestre*), and plant with yellow stargrass (*Hypoxis hirsuta*) for a lovely combination.

The simplest of elements – moss, fallen logs, and deer fern (*Blechnum spicant*) – combine to create a timeless sense of place in this northwestern woodland garden.

SENSITIVE FERN

Onoclea sensibilis

HEIGHT: 2–3 feet (60–90 cm)
BLOOMING PERIOD: non-flowering
EXPOSURE: sun to partial shade

MOISTURE: moist
HABITAT: swamps, meadows, thickets, wet woods
RANGE: prairies and northeast

DESCRIPTION: Unlike other ferns, which are often difficult to identify positively, sensitive fern is very easy to distinguish, and it makes a distinctive addition to the garden. Its thin, papery leaves, which are often a glowing light green (though sometimes darker), have scalloped, wavy edges and turn yellowish early in fall. A creeping fern, sensitive fern is a very rapid spreader when it's content – in moist, rich soil in sun to partial shade – and somewhat less aggressive in average moisture conditions.

MAINTENANCE AND REQUIREMENTS: Sensitive fern's main requirement is moisture, lots of it. Poor drainage is fine, as is neutral to slightly acidic soil. I torture my sensitive fern by growing it in dry soil, but rather than languishing, it gamely puts out fresh fronds to replace the older ones turned crispy . . . it's a trooper. (Just so I'm not arrested by the fern police, I should note that I rescued this plant from a development site, knowing I didn't have ideal conditions, and I'm searching out a more appropriate home for it. I'll replace it with a fern more adapted to dry soil, such as the lovely hay-scented fern [*Dennstaedtia punctilobula*].)

PROPAGATION: Sensitive fern spreads rapidly by creeping rootstocks, so if you've got one plant, you'll have many more soon enough. It's easy to divide in spring or fall. Fertile fronds form beads on the tips of stems in late summer and spores are shed in mid-winter.

GOOD COMPANIONS: Because sensitive fern is so, well, sensitive to early frost, turning yellow and then brown at the first sign of cold, plant it with other moisture-loving species that really come into their own in autumn, such as turtlehead (*Chelone glabra*) and jewelweed (*Impatiens capensis*).

SHARP-LOBED HEPATICA

Hepatica acutiloba

HEIGHT: 4–6 inches (10–15 cm)
BLOOMING PERIOD: early spring
EXPOSURE: shade to partial shade
MOISTURE: moist to dry
HABITAT: woods
RANGE: prairies and northeast

DESCRIPTION: With last year's leaves matted on the ground and looking the worse for wear after a winter's battering, sharp-lobed hepatica sends up small whitish lavender to pink flowers in early spring. Mottled, slightly glossy leaves soon appear, with three pointed lobes. A good plant for dry woodland rock gardens or for along woodland paths.

MAINTENANCE AND REQUIREMENTS: Sharp-lobed hepatica prefers neutral soil, full of organic matter, and can cope with dryish conditions. In semi-shade, it flourishes; with too much sun, the edges of the leaves get crispy.

PROPAGATION: Divide clumps or start from seeds, which ripen in late spring and require cold moist stratification.

GOOD COMPANIONS: In rich, moist woodland conditions, plant with bloodroot (*Sanguinaria canadensis*), white trillium (*Trillium grandiflorum*), false Solomon's seal (*Smilacina racemosa*), blue cohosh (*Caulophyllum thalictroides*), violets (*Viola* spp.), and round-lobed hepatica (*H. americana*).

RELATED SPECIES: Round-lobed hepatica (*H. americana*) is similar in appearance but has round leaves; prefers slightly acidic soil.

SHOWY TICK TREFOIL

Desmodium canadense

HEIGHT: 2–6 feet (60–180 cm)
BLOOMING PERIOD: mid-summer
EXPOSURE: full sun to partial sun
MOISTURE: dry to moist; drought tolerant
HABITAT: open woods, meadows, prairies
RANGE: prairies and northeast

DESCRIPTION: Some people have reservations about using showy tick trefoil in the garden: it can get invasive, its stems aren't strong, and its flowers don't last long (tending to look a bit past it after a week or so). But in a problem area where you want a fast cover, showy tick trefoil is a good choice. The plant is leguminous, and thus fixes nitrogen in the soil; its leaves are attractive, three narrowly oval leaflets; and its flowers are pea-like clusters of pink to purple blooms.

MAINTENANCE AND REQUIREMENTS: Showy tick trefoil is very easy to grow – perhaps too easy for the small garden, where it may take over. Other than needing sun, it is adaptable and versatile, growing in a wide range of soil types, from slightly acidic to neutral soil, sand to clay, and most moisture conditions, from moist to dry.

PROPAGATION: Easy to start from seeds, which mature in elongated, rough pods that stick to clothing and animal fur, an adaptation that ensures this plant travels. Seeds mature in autumn; gently rub the pod with sandpaper for more reliable germination.

GOOD COMPANIONS: In a wild prairie garden, plant with big bluestem (*Andropogon gerardii*) – the tall grass will support the tending-to-flop showy tick trefoil. Also works well with black-eyed Susan (*Rudbeckia hirta*), wild bergamot (*Monarda fistulosa*), and switchgrass (*Panicum virgatum*).

WILDLIFE: Attracts bees and butterflies. Showy tick trefoil is the larval host plant for the silver spotted skipper butterfly and the eastern tailed blue.

SKUNK CABBAGE

Lysichitum americanum

HEIGHT: 12–20 inches (30–50 cm)	**EXPOSURE:** full sun to full shade
BLOOMING PERIOD: early spring	**MOISTURE:** wet to moist
	HABITAT: wet woods, marshes
	RANGE: northwest

DESCRIPTION: This harbinger of spring is a knockout in the pond or in wet woods – don't let its name put you off (though, yes, it is aromatic when in flower – a thick, sweet, slightly but not overpoweringly skunky smell). A brilliant yellow sheath emerges with glorious insistence in early spring and protects the spadix or club, on which minuscule greenish flowers are borne. The shiny leaves are enormous (often 3 feet/90 cm long or more and 1 1/2 feet/45 cm wide).

MAINTENANCE AND REQUIREMENTS: The native habitat of skunk cabbage – wet woods – gives two important clues about its requirements: it needs plenty of moisture (indeed, saturated soil or complete submersion) and nutrient-rich soil. Give it lots of room, and don't worry if it goes dormant in mid- to late summer – it will be back.

PROPAGATION: Sow the fleshy, pulpy seeds as soon as they ripen in summer. They'll germinate well but seedlings grow slowly. You can also divide established plants.

GOOD COMPANIONS: In wet woods, plant with lady fern (*Athyrium filix-femina*) and false hellebore (*Veratrum viride*). Near water, plant with western swamp laurel (*Kalmia microphylla*) and marsh marigold (*Caltha biflora*).

RELATED SPECIES: Though not related, the eastern skunk cabbage (*Symplocarpus foetidus*) is very similar in habitat and behavior, but its shell-like spathe is a gorgeous mottled purple-brown.

MISCELLANY: Sometimes called swamp lantern.

SMALL-FLOWERED ALUMROOT

Heuchera micrantha

HEIGHT: 6–24 inches (15–60 cm)
BLOOMING PERIOD: summer
EXPOSURE: partial shade to full sun
MOISTURE: moist to average
HABITAT: streambanks, rocky crevices, forest edge
RANGE: northwest

Small-flowered alumroot (lower left and upper right) with lomatium (center)

DESCRIPTION: A billowy cloud of small white flowers on wiry stalks makes this plant a knockout in summer – there are hundreds of flowers on each plant. Leaves are maple-like, with coarse teeth, and sometimes turn reddish in autumn. Stems are hairy.

MAINTENANCE AND REQUIREMENTS: Small-flowered alumroot is easy to please and spreads rapidly in partial shade to full sun, moist to average soil.

PROPAGATION: Easy to propagate from seeds, which should be scattered on soil surface in autumn, or by rhizome cutting or division in spring or autumn.

GOOD COMPANIONS: Looks good with lomatium (*Lomatium nudicaule*), wood sorrel (*Oxalis oregana*), and inside-out flower (*Vancouveria hexandra*).

RELATED SPECIES: Northwest species include round-leaved alumroot (*H. cylindrica*) with creamy yellowish white, bell-shaped flowers, and smooth alumroot (*H. glabra*), which is good for rock gardens. For the prairies, try alumroot (*H. richardsonii*), with small greenish or purplish flowers. In the northeast, try *H. americana*, with its tall flowering stalks (2 to 3 feet/60 to 90 cm) and small green, pink or purple bell-shaped flowers.

SOLOMON'S SEAL

Polygonatum biflorum

HEIGHT: 1–3 feet (30–90 cm)
BLOOMING PERIOD: mid- to late spring
EXPOSURE: deep shade to partial sun

MOISTURE: dry to moist
HABITAT: woods and thickets
RANGE: prairies and northeast

DESCRIPTION: Solomon's seal does extra duty in all departments as a trouble-free, tall-growing foliage plant with interest throughout the seasons. The insistent way it pokes through the earth in early spring with fleshy shoots; its charming greenish white bell-shaped flowers, which dangle along arching stems; its luminous green foliage in summer; and its blue-black berries in fall – all make this a choice plant. Solomon's seal works well around the base of trees.

MAINTENANCE AND REQUIREMENTS: Versatile in its requirements, Solomon's seal will grow in deep to light shade, acidic to neutral soil, in dry to moist conditions, but it does best in rich woodland soil.

PROPAGATION: Solomon's seal spreads by underground rhizomes; propagate by rhizome division in early spring or fall. If planting seeds, don't let them dry out – plant when fresh.

GOOD COMPANIONS: Any of the rich woodland denizens look good with Solomon's seal, especially blue cohosh (*Caulophyllum thalictroides*), white trillium (*Trillium grandiflorum*), sharp-lobed hepatica (*Hepatica acutiloba*), and bloodroot (*Sanguinaria canadensis*).

RELATED SPECIES: Great Solomon's seal (*P. canaliculatum*) is taller (5 feet/150 cm) with larger flowers.

SPIDERWORT

Tradescantia virginiana

HEIGHT: 8–24 inches (20–60 cm)

BLOOMING PERIOD: spring to early summer

EXPOSURE: sun to light shade

MOISTURE: dry to moist

HABITAT: woodland edges, thickets, meadows

RANGE: prairies and northeast

DESCRIPTION: The flowers of spiderwort are very simple-looking, but their blue just glows. The leaves are also interesting – long and iris-like, they're folded in the middle, producing a kind of channel. Although the plant can grow to 2 feet (60 cm), the leaves tend to drape down rather than stand erect, giving a mound-ish effect.

MAINTENANCE AND REQUIREMENTS: Spiderwort is very adaptable and will grow in a wide range of soils, from moist to dry, clay to sand. It's also versatile in its light requirements, doing well in full sun to more shaded conditions. Deadhead to extend blooming or cut the whole plant back in early summer to encourage a late-summer second flowering.

PROPAGATION: Easy to start from seeds, which ripen in late summer. Can also be divided in spring or fall.

GOOD COMPANIONS: Plant with nodding wild onion (*Allium cernuum*), evening primrose (*Oenothera biennis*), New Jersey tea (*Ceanothus americanus*), and lance-leaved coreopsis (*Coreopsis lanceolata*) for an attractive blue, yellow, and white combination. In open woodland conditions, plant with tall meadowrue (*Thalictrum polygamum*), wild geranium (*Geranium maculatum*), and columbine (*Aquilegia canadensis*).

RELATED SPECIES: A related spiderwort for the prairie region is Ohio spiderwort (*T. ohiensis*).

WILDLIFE: Attracts butterflies.

Spotted Joe-pye weed (left and right) with ironweed (center)

SPOTTED JOE-PYE WEED

Eupatorium maculatum

HEIGHT: 3–10 feet (.9–3 m)	**MOISTURE:** moist to average
BLOOMING PERIOD: summer to fall	**HABITAT:** damp meadows, thickets
EXPOSURE: full sun to filtered sunlight	**RANGE:** prairies and northeast

DESCRIPTION: Spotted Joe-pye weed is a great example of a common wild plant that would be oohed and aahed over if it were a rare exotic – but because it's a roadside "weed," we rarely give it the praise it deserves. So tune up the trumpets: Joe-pye weed is a brassy beauty. Growing tall – 6 feet (180 cm) is common – with whorled leaves along the sturdy stem, it's the huge cluster of purple to pink fuzzy flowers that make this plant a knockout. After blooming for a few weeks in mid-summer, the big globes turn brown – and still look interesting.

MAINTENANCE AND REQUIREMENTS: Although it prefers moist conditions (and is thus perfect for a poorly drained problem area), Joe-pye weed will also do just fine in average conditions – and I grow mine in dry soil (the leaves go a bit droopy in drought, but perk up with the next rain). One particularly low-maintenance feature of this plant is that despite its height, it never needs staking. In nutrient-poor or sandy soil, it won't grow as large. Slightly acidic to neutral soil.

PROPAGATION: Joe-pye weed is easy to start from seeds, which mature in fall. Young plants will quickly spread on their own, filling whatever space you give them. Plant can also be divided in early spring or in fall.

GOOD COMPANIONS: At the back of a moist border, plant with boneset (*Eupatorium perfoliatum*), tall ironweed (*Vernonia altissima*), Queen of the prairie (*Filipendula rubra*), and swamp milkweed (*Asclepias incarnata*). In average moisture conditions, it serves as a good supporting plant for yellow coneflower (*Ratibida pinnata*) and looks good with grass-leaved goldenrod (*Solidago graminifolia*) and sweet black-eyed Susan (*Rudbeckia subtomentosa*).

RELATED SPECIES: Sweet Joe-pye weed (*E. purpureum*) looks very similar and grows in similar conditions, but has a somewhat rounder flower cluster. See entry for boneset (*E. perfoliatum*).

SPRING BEAUTY

Claytonia virginica

HEIGHT: 6 inches (15 cm)
BLOOMING PERIOD: early spring
EXPOSURE: partial shade
MOISTURE: moist to average
HABITAT: woods
RANGE: prairies and northeast

DESCRIPTION: One of the earliest plants to announce spring, this appropriately named plant is a tiny charmer. Leaves are narrow and the small flowers are white to pink, with darker pink veins. Put it close to the front of the border, so you won't miss its delicate show. Spring beauty goes dormant in summer, but because of its small size doesn't leave an unmanageable gap – any nearby plants will quickly fill in the space.

MAINTENANCE AND REQUIREMENTS: Spring beauty requires rich woodland soil, full of organic matter, and will do well in the partial shade of the early-spring woodland. Acidic to neutral soil. Add compost to the soil before planting.

PROPAGATION: Can be started from seeds, which should be planted fresh, when they mature in early summer.

GOOD COMPANIONS: Plant with sharp-lobed hepatica (*Hepatica acutiloba*), goldenseal (*Hydrastis canadensis*), violets (*Viola* spp.), mayapple (*Podophyllum peltatum*), and wood anemone (*Anemone quinquefolia*).

RELATED SPECIES: Carolina spring beauty (*C. caroliniana*) looks very similar but has wider leaves. In the prairies and northwest, try *C. lanceolata*, which grows very low (3 inches/8 cm) and has white flowers in spring.

This northeastern meadow garden was designed to attract butterflies. Native species include liatris (*Liatris spicata*) and, in the back left, spotted Joe-pye weed (*Eupatorium maculatum*). Non-natives include both the white and yellow yarrow (*Achillea*).

STIFF GOLDENROD

Solidago rigida

HEIGHT: 1–5 feet (30–150 cm)
BLOOMING PERIOD: late summer
EXPOSURE: full sun
MOISTURE: average to dry; drought tolerant
HABITAT: prairies, meadows
RANGE: prairies and northeast

DESCRIPTION: Not a very attractive name (the "stiff" refers to the rigid leaves) for a very attractive species of goldenrod. It does not get bushy, its leaves clasping tight to the stem, but its flat-topped flower heads are dense with dark yellow blooms.

MAINTENANCE AND REQUIREMENTS: Stiff goldenrod requires nothing in the way of care. In sun, in dry to average soil, clay to sand, nutrient-poor conditions, acidic to neutral, it will do fine. May get mold on the leaves; cutting it back or dividing the plant will help.

PROPAGATION: Easy to start from seeds, which require cold moist stratification, or by dividing plants in spring or fall.

GOOD COMPANIONS: Stiff goldenrod looks great with the dried seedheads of New York ironweed (*Vernonia noveboracensis*) and blue vervain (*Verbena hastata*). Combine with other late-summer bloomers such as obedient plant (*Physostegia virginiana*) and New England aster (*Aster novae-angliae*).

RELATED SPECIES: There are many gorgeous goldenrods from which to choose: grass-leaved goldenrod (*S. graminifolia*), which can be invasive, blue-stemmed goldenrod (*S. caesia*), showy goldenrod (*S. speciosa*), and rough-stemmed goldenrod (*S. rugosa*) are just a few. In the northwest, try the alpine species, northern goldenrod (*S. multiradiata*), a low grower with clusters of yellow flowers, or narrow goldenrod (*S. spathulata*), which grows 1 to 3 feet (30 to 90 cm). See entry for zig zag goldenrod (*S. flexicaulis*).

MISCELLANY: Despite what too many people think, goldenrod does not aggravate hayfever – ragweed is the culprit.

SWAMP MILKWEED

Asclepias incarnata

HEIGHT: 2–4 feet (60–120 cm)	**HABITAT:** thickets, wet meadows, and moist prairies
BLOOMING PERIOD: summer	
EXPOSURE: full sun	**RANGE:** prairies and northeast
MOISTURE: moist to average	

DESCRIPTION: "Swamp" and "weed" – two superficial strikes against this plant, if one were evaluating it only by name. But don't let such things put you off, as swamp milkweed is a great plant. Its deep red to pink long-lasting flowers are clustered at the top of tall stems and emit an intoxicating fragrance of vanilla. Leaves are willow-like.

MAINTENANCE AND REQUIREMENTS: A plant of wet meadows and therefore preferring moist conditions, milkweed also thrives in average soil. (One year, a young plant of mine was demolished by aphids, and I'm sure it was weakened and thus vulnerable to attack because of my dry soil. Not a tragedy – the new plants are now strong – but a warning about pushing it.) Swamp milkweed is also versatile with regard to nutrient requirements and pH, doing just fine in a wide range.

PROPAGATION: Easy to start from seeds, which mature in early autumn, or by dividing established plants in spring.

GOOD COMPANIONS: For a succession of blooms, plant with tall meadowrue (*Thalictrum polygamum*), which has billowy white flowers in summer, boneset (*Eupatorium perfoliatum*), and New England aster (*Aster novae-angliae*). In a very wet place, try combining with a native sedge such as wool grass (*Scirpus cyperinus*).

RELATED SPECIES: See entry for butterfly weed (*A. tuberosa*).

WILDLIFE: Plants in the milkweed family are the only known larval food for the monarch butterfly; also larval host plant for the queen butterfly. Swamp milkweed attracts many different butterflies to its nectar.

SWORD FERN

Polystichum munitum

HEIGHT: 2–3 feet (60–90 cm)
BLOOMING PERIOD: non-flowering
EXPOSURE: full shade to partial sun

MOISTURE: moist to average; drought tolerant in summer
HABITAT: conifer forests
RANGE: northwest

DESCRIPTION: Sword fern is the signature plant for Pacific Northwest woodland gardens. An evergreen, it grows tall, with spiky fronds in circular clumps and many finely toothed leaflets. Ideal for a large area you don't want to worry about maintaining, sword fern spreads rapidly, creating a rainforest garden all on its own.

MAINTENANCE AND REQUIREMENTS: Although it prefers rich, moist soil, sword fern is a very adaptable plant and will grow in the drier summer conditions typical of the northwest. It's happy in full shade to partial sun, clay to loam, but requires acidic soil.

PROPAGATION: Sword fern will spread merrily on its own, but you can also divide plants in fall, which is a much faster method of propagation than starting plants from collected spores.

GOOD COMPANIONS: A dense bed of sword fern under the dappled canopy of vine maple looks great. Its drought tolerance in summer also makes it a good choice as a groundcover under the drying shade of conifers. Other good companions include Canada mayflower (*Maianthemum dilatatum*), wood sorrel (*Oxalis oregana*), candy flower (*Montia sibirica*), and western bleeding heart (*Dicentra formosa*).

RELATED SPECIES: In the Rocky Mountains and northwest, try Anderson's holly fern (*P. andersonii*) or mountain holly fern (*P. lonchitis*). For the northeast, see entry for Christmas fern (*P. acrostichoides*).

TROUT LILY

Erythronium americanum

HEIGHT: 4–10 inches (10–25 cm)	**MOISTURE:** moist to dry
BLOOMING PERIOD: early spring	**HABITAT:** rich woods
	RANGE: prairies and northeast
EXPOSURE: shade to filtered sun	

DESCRIPTION: Also known as adder's tongue and dog-tooth violet (though it's in the lily family), this plant is a familiar harbinger of spring. Its two brownish mottled leaves carpet woodlands and its nodding yellow flowers are a beautiful sight. Plant in masses, interspersed with other woodlanders that will fill in the gaps when this spring ephemeral goes dormant in early summer.

MAINTENANCE AND REQUIREMENTS: Trout lily requires rich woodland soil, full of organic matter, slightly acidic to neutral (pH 5 to 6), moist to dry. Dig in lots of compost before planting.

PROPAGATION: Can be started from seeds, which should be planted fresh in summer, though plants will take many years to flower. Divide root offshoots in fall (mark the plant in spring, pre-dormancy).

GOOD COMPANIONS: Plant with white trillium (*Trillium grandiflorum*), cut-leaved toothwort (*Dentaria laciniata*), twinleaf (*Jeffersonia diphylla*), and wild ginger (*Asarum canadense*).

RELATED SPECIES: In the prairie region, try prairie trout lily (*E. mesochoreum*), which has delicate whitish purple flowers and grows in full sun, or white trout lily (*E. albidum*), which grows in woodlands. For northwest gardens, see entry for white fawn lily (*E. oregonum*).

MISCELLANY: Make sure your source guarantees nursery propagation.

TWINFLOWER

Linnaea borealis

HEIGHT: 4 inches (10 cm)
BLOOMING PERIOD: late spring through summer
EXPOSURE: sun to partial shade

MOISTURE: moist to average
HABITAT: woodland, forest margin
RANGE: northwest, Rocky Mountains, and prairies

DESCRIPTION: Great as a groundcover in the woodland garden, twinflower's shiny evergreen foliage carpets the ground. Whitish pink, funnel-shaped, fragrant flowers appear in late spring through summer.

MAINTENANCE AND REQUIREMENTS: Twinflower needs good drainage but will grow in sun to partial shade, as long as the soil is moist (the plant is intolerant of drought). Give it room to spread.

PROPAGATION: The easiest way to propagate twinflower is either by taking cuttings in summer or by layering the plant (bend a branch to the ground, in a shallow trench, cover it with a bit of soil, hold it down if necessary with some wire, and the plant will root; cut it away from the parent when rooted, and transplant).

GOOD COMPANIONS: Plant with bunchberry (*Cornus canadensis*) for a great spring show. Other good companions include sword fern (*Polystichum munitum*), vanilla leaf (*Achlys triphylla*), western trillium (*Trillium ovatum*), and shrubs such as red-flowering currant (*Ribes sanguineum*), salal (*Gaultheria shallon*), Indian plum (*Oemleria cerasiformis*), and vine maple (*Acer circinatum*).

VANILLA LEAF

Achlys triphylla

HEIGHT: 1 foot (30 cm)	**MOISTURE:** moist to average
BLOOMING PERIOD: spring	**HABITAT:** coniferous forests
EXPOSURE: deep to partial shade	**RANGE:** northwest

DESCRIPTION: These simple leaves make quite a show: divided into threes, they support a single wiry stem that pokes up in mid-spring, a spike covered in small white flowers. The leaves' light green color is beautiful, especially when they form an extensive cover.

MAINTENANCE AND REQUIREMENTS: Vanilla leaf prefers moist, well-drained, slightly acidic soil in deep to partial shade. However, give it a try in the dry shade of Douglas fir.

PROPAGATION: Start from seed or divide rhizomes.

GOOD COMPANIONS: Good companions include sword fern (*Polystichum munitum*), inside-out flower (*Vancouveria hexandra*), and oak fern (*Gymnocarpium dryopteris*). A lovely combination includes vanilla leaf, western trillium (*Trillium ovatum*), and starflower (*Trientalis latifolia*).

MISCELLANY: Leaves give off a vanilla fragrance when dry.

VIRGINIA BLUEBELLS

Mertensia virginica

HEIGHT: 1–2 feet (30–60 cm)
BLOOMING PERIOD: spring
EXPOSURE: partial shade to filtered sunlight

MOISTURE: average to moist
HABITAT: woods
RANGE: northeast and prairies

DESCRIPTION: I'm a broken record on the subject of blue: give me more, more, more. Though the buds of Virginia bluebells start out pink, they open to a luscious blue, covering the plant with drooping, pendulous trumpet-shaped blooms. The leaves also do chameleon tricks, starting out purple then changing to a light green. This spring ephemeral, alas, goes dormant in summer, but it's a heavenly blue while it lasts.

MAINTENANCE AND REQUIREMENTS: Moist fertile soil is best, but Virginia bluebells will do fine in average moisture conditions as long as the soil is high in organic material. Give it room to grow into large clumps.

PROPAGATION: Start from seed collected in early summer, just as the plant is going dormant. Or divide rhizomes when the plant is dormant.

GOOD COMPANIONS: As far as I'm concerned, yellow was invented to make blue even better. Mix with large-flowered bellwort (*Uvularia grandiflora*), wood poppy (*Stylophorum diphyllum*), and tall meadowrue (*Thalictrum polygamum*) for a lovely combo. Or, for a white and blue combination, plant Virginia bluebells with a groundcover of foamflower (*Tiarella cordifolia*) – not only do they look good together, but the groundcover will fill in the holes left when Virginia bluebells go dormant. Ferns will also do the trick.

RELATED SPECIES: Tall lungwort (*M. paniculata*) grows from the prairies west, has deep blue drooping flower clusters, and blooms in early summer. A Rocky Mountain species is mountain bluebells (*M. ciliata*), which has similar requirements. Both look great with yellow fawn lily (*Erythronium grandiflorum*).

MISCELLANY: Because they're often dug from the wild (an ethical no-no), don't buy these unless your nursery source can guarantee that the plants are nursery propagated.

In late summer, the northeastern meadow garden bursts with color: brown-eyed Susan (*Rudbeckia triloba*), middleground, heart-leaved aster (*Aster cordifolius*), foreground, and the feathery seed plumes of fireweed (*Epilobium angustifolium*), background.

VIRGINIA CREEPER

Parthenocissus vitacea

HEIGHT: n/a	**MOISTURE:** moist to dry
BLOOMING PERIOD: summer	**HABITAT:** woods, thickets
EXPOSURE: sun to shade	**RANGE:** northeast

DESCRIPTION: Virginia creeper is an extremely versatile vine that has many uses in the garden: it can be grown up a rough wall, fence, or trellis, providing a quick cover, and it can be used as a fast-growing groundcover in a woodland planting. It is invasive, though, crowding out other species, so use it only where you want nothing else to grow. Leaves are a glossy green throughout the summer, then turn a striking red in autumn. Flowers (greenish clusters) are not showy, but the fruits in late summer to fall are bright blue berries.

MAINTENANCE AND REQUIREMENTS: Virginia creeper grows in sun to shade, moist to dryish conditions, and is not demanding in nutrients needed. It attaches itself to vertical surfaces with slender twining tendrils, so it does require some form of support (netting will do) if you want it to grow up a smooth wall.

PROPAGATION: You can start Virginia creeper from seed, but a much faster method of propagation is to take stem cuttings in summer or to layer the vine (let it ramble along the soil surface and the vine will put down roots at a number of places; you can dig up these rooted sections – cutting them away from the parent plant – and plant them elsewhere).

GOOD COMPANIONS: Jim Hodgins, the editor of *Wildflower* magazine, has used Virginia creeper with cunning effectiveness to cover a utility pole outside his house. After hanging fine netting over the pole, he planted Virginia creeper and an annual self-seeding vine; the vine's flowers poke out from the dark green of the Virginia creeper and the whole thing looks like a huge shaggy creature that's landed on the sidewalk.

RELATED SPECIES: Another very closely related species, *P. quinquefolia*, has small adhesive discs at the tips of its tendrils (almost like little suction cups), so it is able to clasp onto smooth surfaces and thus does not require a trellis or netting.

VIRGINIA MOUNTAIN MINT

✺

Pycnanthemum virginianum

HEIGHT: 2–3 feet (60–90 cm)
BLOOMING PERIOD: mid- to late summer
EXPOSURE: full sun to filtered sunlight
MOISTURE: moist to dry
HABITAT: dry to moist prairies
RANGE: prairies and northeast

DESCRIPTION: Rather aggressive, Virginia mountain mint quickly spreads to fill in large areas, but who can complain when its delicate white flowers, in heavy clusters at the top of square stems, are so attractive and long-lasting? Its aromatic leaves are lance-shaped and narrow, on many-branched stems.

MAINTENANCE AND REQUIREMENTS: Virginia mountain mint will flourish with little care in neutral soil, in moist to dry conditions. (It is less aggressive in dry soil.) You may need to control its spread by digging up volunteers and passing them along to other gardeners.

PROPAGATION: Divide plants, which spread by rhizomes, in spring. Young seedlings are easy to recognize because of their square stems – characteristic of plants in the mint family. Tip cuttings, taken in early summer, will also root.

GOOD COMPANIONS: I like to combine aggressive species and let them fight it out – hence my planting of Virginia mountain mint and sundrops (*Oenothera fruticosa*). Other good companions include blue vervain (*Verbena hastata*), cardinal flower (*Lobelia cardinalis*), butterfly weed (*Asclepias tuberosa*), stiff goldenrod (*Solidago rigida*), black-eyed Susan (*Rudbeckia hirta*), and liatris (*Liatris* spp.).

RELATED SPECIES: The later-blooming narrow-leaved mountain mint (*P. tenuifolium*) grows up to 3 feet (90 cm) in very dry soil, and blooms in summer. Hoary mountain mint (*P. incanum*) grows 1 to 3 feet (30 to 90 cm) and has small whitish lavender flowers in mid- to late summer.

WILDLIFE: Attracts butterflies.

VIRGINIA WATERLEAF

Hydrophyllum virginianum

Virginia waterleaf (middle) with trillium (bottom left) and false Solomon's seal (top right)

HEIGHT: 1–2½ feet (30–75 cm)

BLOOMING PERIOD: spring

EXPOSURE: full shade to partial shade

MOISTURE: moist to average

HABITAT: moist woods and clearings

RANGE: northeast

DESCRIPTION: If you've got a large, moist, shady area and you want to plant an aggressive grower, Virginia waterleaf is a good choice. The lavender bell-shaped flowers, appearing in spring, aren't particularly showy, but they do have an understated grace.

MAINTENANCE AND REQUIREMENTS: Virginia waterleaf requires rich, moist soil in full to partial shade, and in such conditions can become invasive.

PROPAGATION: Sow ripe seeds, which mature in summer, for germination the next spring. Rhizome can also be divided in fall.

GOOD COMPANIONS: Because Virginia waterleaf is not particularly showy, you may want to interplant some more interesting moisture-loving species to give a bit of a blast to the whole arrangement: turk's-cap lily (*Lilium superbum*), for example, will rise dramatically out of the waterleaf foliage to 6 or 7 feet (1.8 to 2 m). It also looks good with mayapple (*Podophyllum peltatum*) and wild ginger (*Asarum canadense*).

RELATED SPECIES: Appendaged waterleaf (*H. appendiculatum*) is very similar, with pale violet flowers, but the leaves are maple-like. Broad-leaved waterleaf (*H. canadense*) grows to 18 inches (45 cm) and has white to pink flowers and maple-like leaves. In the northwest, in a woodland garden, try *H. fendleri*, 1 to 3 feet (30 to 90 cm), with white flowers, or Pacific waterleaf (*H. tenuipes*), 1 to 3 feet (30 to 90 cm), with purple flowers.

VIRGIN'S BOWER

Clematis virginiana

HEIGHT: n/a	**MOISTURE:** moist to dry
BLOOMING PERIOD: summer to fall	**HABITAT:** woodland edges, thickets
EXPOSURE: full sun to partial shade	**RANGE:** prairies and northeast

DESCRIPTION: Virgin's bower is a fantastic vine, especially for problem areas, such as dry, partially shaded sites, because it is aggressive and fast growing. It covers a huge area in just one season and will self-sow throughout the garden (it also sets down roots wherever the vine touches the ground). Flowers are white billowy clouds throughout the summer, and its seedheads are also great – wispy plumes.

MAINTENANCE AND REQUIREMENTS: This vine attaches itself to surfaces with twisted stems, rather than tendrils, so it needs the support of a lattice or similar structure. It will grow in moist, average, or dry soil, in full sun to partial shade. Be vigilant about weeding out volunteers, otherwise they will take over the garden.

PROPAGATION: You can start from seeds, but a much faster method is layering: simply bend the vine onto the surface of the soil, secure it with wire, and pretty soon, a new plant will be rooted, and you can cut it away from the parent.

GOOD COMPANIONS: In front of a sunny trellised wall covered in virgin's bower, plant colorful meadow or prairie species such as culver's root (*Veronicastrum virginicum*), false sunflower (*Heliopsis helianthoides*), and New York ironweed (*Vernonia noveboracensis*).

RELATED SPECIES: In the prairies, try western clematis (*C. ligusticifolia*), which has white flowers, or purple clematis (*C. verticellaris*). In the northwest, try rock clematis (*C. columbiana*), which is drought tolerant and has blue flowers, or white clematis (*C. ligusticifolia*).

MISCELLANY: In a bizarre example of internal contradiction, virgin's bower is also known as old man's beard.

WESTERN BLEEDING HEART

Dicentra formosa

HEIGHT: 8–18 inches (20–45 cm)
BLOOMING PERIOD: early to late spring, into summer
EXPOSURE: filtered sunlight, partial to full shade
MOISTURE: moist to average
HABITAT: moist woodlands
RANGE: northwest

DESCRIPTION: Although the flowers are quite attractive (pink and heart-shaped, they hang down in clusters that nod in the breeze), it's the lacy fern-like foliage of this plant that makes it so appealing. Leaves are bluish green. Very useful in an understory planting in deep shade; spreads rapidly.

MAINTENANCE AND REQUIREMENTS: In the wild, bleeding heart grows in rich, moist woods so it does best in similar conditions, but don't let regular moisture conditions stop you from trying it in the garden, as long as soil is nutrient-rich and full of organic material.

PROPAGATION: Easy to grow from seeds, which mature in summer; plant fresh. Rhizomes can be divided in early spring or mid-summer, after flowering.

GOOD COMPANIONS: Looks attractive with wood sorrel (*Oxalis oregana*).

RELATED SPECIES: Golden corydalis (*Corydalis aurea*), also in the bleeding heart family, has that same ferny foliage, but the flowers are yellow. For northeast species, see entry for Dutchman's breeches (*D. cucullaria*).

WILDLIFE: Ants do good work for this plant in dispersing the seeds. Attracts butterflies. Larval host plant for the clodius parnassian butterfly.

MISCELLANY: Also known as Pacific bleeding heart.

WESTERN TRILLIUM

Trillium ovatum

HEIGHT: 4–16 inches (10–40 cm)	**MOISTURE:** moist to average
BLOOMING PERIOD: spring	**HABITAT:** moist woods
EXPOSURE: full shade to partial shade	**RANGE:** northwest and Rocky Mountains

DESCRIPTION: In the spring, woodland gardens come alive with the appearance of showy trilliums. Their single white flowers are enchantingly simple, and their leaves, a whorl of three at the top of the stem, with the flower perched on top, are attractive. The white flowers turn pinkish with age.

MAINTENANCE AND REQUIREMENTS: Trilliums are rich woods denizens and thus in the garden they require soil that's full of organic matter. Another important requirement is moisture and good drainage – don't let them dry out. Colonies of trilliums are slow to increase, but worth the wait.

PROPAGATION: Although they will take years to flower, trilliums can be propagated from seeds (contained in pulpy fruits), collected and planted fresh in late summer to fall – be patient (above-ground growth may not appear for two seasons) and be careful not to disturb young seedlings.

GOOD COMPANIONS: Looks good with wild ginger (*Asarum caudatum*), fairy bells (*Disporum hookeri*), and false Solomon's seal (*Smilacina racemosa*).

RELATED SPECIES: In the northeast and prairie regions, there are many trilliums to choose from: the white trillium (*T. grandiflorum*), which grows to 1 foot (30 cm); nodding trillium (*T. cernuum*), with white to pinkish flowers that hang down; purple trillium (*T. erectum*), which has rich maroon flowers; and toadshade trillium (*T. sessile*), with a red flower (there is also a yellow form) that appears to be closed because its petals are so erect.

WILDLIFE: Ants distribute the seeds.

MISCELLANY: Often wild-dug, make sure your source guarantees plants are nursery propagated. Also known as wakerobin.

WHITE FAWN LILY

Erythronium oregonum

HEIGHT: 4–18 inches (10–45 cm)	**MOISTURE:** average to moist
BLOOMING PERIOD: early to late spring	**HABITAT:** moist meadows, open woods
EXPOSURE: full sun to partial shade	**RANGE:** northwest

DESCRIPTION: A moist meadow carpeted with these beauties in spring is an arresting sight. White flowers, yellow at the base, hang down from the stem, but turn up at the end. Leaves are glossy green, mottled with pale green and dark brown.

MAINTENANCE AND REQUIREMENTS: Provide well-drained, acidic to slightly acidic fertile soil in full sun to partial shade and let them spread (alas, slowly). Mulch with compost. Slugs may be a problem – hand pick them.

PROPAGATION: Seeds take a long time to reach flowering, from three to six years. Bulbs should be planted deep – approximately 4 inches (10 cm) – and not be allowed to dry out prior to planting.

GOOD COMPANIONS: Plant with broad-leaved shooting star (*Dodecatheon hendersonii*) for a glorious combination in moist meadows. In open woods, plant with western bleeding heart (*Dicentra formosa*) and false Solomon's seal (*Smilacina racemosa*).

RELATED SPECIES: In the northwest, try pink fawn lily (*E. revolutum*) in moist, open to dense shade; glacier fawn lily (*E. montanum*), which has white flowers and needs moisture; and yellow glacier lily (*E. grandiflorum*), a Rocky Mountain species for rich, moist sites. For northeast species, see entry for trout lily (*E. americanum*).

WILDLIFE: Attracts bees.

MISCELLANY: Sometimes called Easter Lily, which just confuses things. Make sure your nursery guarantees that these bulbs have not been dug from the wild.

WHITE WOOD ASTER

Aster divaricatus

HEIGHT: 1–3 feet (30–90 cm)
BLOOMING PERIOD: mid- to late summer
EXPOSURE: shade to partial shade
MOISTURE: dry to average
HABITAT: dry woods
RANGE: northeast

DESCRIPTION: Another understated plant for dry woodland gardens, white wood aster has largish heart-shaped leaves and flat-topped clusters of white flowers that bloom throughout the summer. Considered weedy by some, I view the white wood aster's generous volunteering as a gift. In dry shade, one needs take-over-ish plants.

MAINTENANCE AND REQUIREMENTS: White wood aster requires very little in the way of care; it's vigorous, even aggressive, in dry soil, shade to partial shade, slightly acidic to neutral conditions.

PROPAGATION: You can start it from seeds, which mature in late fall, by dividing clumps in early spring, or you can just allow it to spread on its own.

GOOD COMPANIONS: A very colorful and long-lasting combination for partially shaded, dry woodlands is white wood aster with brown-eyed Susan (*Rudbeckia triloba*). It grows well with columbine (*Aquilegia canadensis*), another woodlander that tolerates dry soil.

RELATED SPECIES: Another good aster for dry shady woodland gardens is large-leaved aster (*A. macrophyllus*), which grows 2 to 5 feet (60 to 150 cm), has light blue (sometimes white) flowers in late summer into fall, and massive (4 to 8 inches/10 to 20 cm wide) basal leaves. In open woods in the northwest, try Engelmann's aster (*A. engelmannii*), which has white flowers, with yellow centers, and grows 1 1/2 to 5 feet (45 to 150 cm). See entry for New England aster (*A. novae-angliae*).

The evergreen northwestern shrub Oregon grape (*Mahonia aquifolium*) complements a woodland planting, putting on a bright show in spring, then producing tart purple berries, which can be made into jelly.

WILD BERGAMOT

Monarda fistulosa

HEIGHT: 2–4 feet (60–120 cm)
BLOOMING PERIOD: summer
EXPOSURE: full sun
MOISTURE: average to dry; drought tolerant

HABITAT: prairies, old fields, thickets
RANGE: prairies and northeast

DESCRIPTION: A signature plant of the prairie or meadow garden, wild bergamot is a must-have. Lavender to purple jester-hat–shaped flowers appear in early summer and last for weeks. Leaves emit that wonderful Earl Grey tea smell when crushed.

MAINTENANCE AND REQUIREMENTS: Wild bergamot is very easy to look after, requiring nothing in the way of special care. A versatile plant, it can be grown in most soil types, from clay to sand, in moist to dry conditions, fertile to nutrient poor. The only problem you're likely to run into is powdery mildew on the leaves. Try to open up some space around the clump or divide the crowded, mature plant. You can also prune moldy foliage and new growth will appear. Deadhead flowers to extend the blooming period.

PROPAGATION: Very easy to start from seeds, which ripen in autumn; seeds do not require cold stratification.

You can also propagate by dividing mature clumps in early spring – a good idea, anyway, to improve air circulation and keep plant vigorous (center of clumps tends to die back as the plant ages).

GOOD COMPANIONS: Wild bergamot is the mainstay in many attractive prairie combinations in the first half of the summer. It looks great with Virginia mountain mint (*Pycnanthemum virginianum*), black-eyed Susan (*Rudbeckia hirta*), culver's root (*Veronicastrum virginicum*), rattlesnake master (*Eryngium yuccifolium*), wild indigo (*Baptisia tinctoria*), and false sunflower (*Heliopsis helianthoides*).

RELATED SPECIES: Spotted horsemint (*M. punctata*), which grows 3 feet (90 cm) tall, has pale yellow flowers, spotted with purple.

WILDLIFE: Attracts butterflies, hummingbirds, and bees. Food plant for larval gray hairstreak butterfly.

WILD COLUMBINE

Aquilegia formosa

HEIGHT: 1–3 feet (30–90 cm)
BLOOMING PERIOD: late spring to early summer
EXPOSURE: sun to partial shade

MOISTURE: dry to average
HABITAT: dry woods, disturbed clearings
RANGE: northwest

DESCRIPTION: Many exotic cultivars are available in the nursery trade, but for my money, the wild columbine can't be beat. Its red tubular flowers, 1 inch (2.5 cm) long, with tinges of yellow and five spurs, hang from the stalk. An airy and delicate-looking addition to the edges of a woodland garden or rock garden.

MAINTENANCE AND REQUIREMENTS: Columbine grows well in nutrient-poor, neutral soil on the dry side, in sun to partial shade. Leaf miners often tunnel through the leaves, leaving tell-tale markings, but don't do serious damage to the plant (explain their white tracings as just one more design feature if anyone asks).

PROPAGATION: Columbine self-seeds with abandon – seedlings pop up around the parent plant throughout the summer and can be moved the next spring, after they've proved their hardiness. Sow seeds in spring, summer, or fall and rake in.

GOOD COMPANIONS: Columbine looks great with arnica (*Arnica amplexicaules*) and *Penstemon fruticosus*. Also try with cinquefoil (*Potentilla gracilis*).

RELATED SPECIES: The northeastern species (*A. canadensis*) is similar in appearance and requirements. Colorado columbine (*A. coerulea*) is the state flower of Colorado and is completely stunning – sky blue and white. Another blue species, the small-flowered columbine (*A. brevistyla*), is good for prairie gardens.

WILDLIFE: Hummingbirds feed on the nectar of wild columbine. Also attracts bees and moths.

Wild geranium (center) with foamflower

WILD GERANIUM

Geranium maculatum

HEIGHT: 1–2 feet (30–60 cm)	**MOISTURE:** dry to moist
BLOOMING PERIOD: late spring and early summer	**HABITAT:** deciduous woods
EXPOSURE: partial shade to sun	**RANGE:** prairies and northeast

DESCRIPTION: Loose clusters of small (1 inch/2.5 cm) but numerous and long-lasting lavender to blue flowers are a nice sight in the spring woodland garden. The foliage is also attractive: deeply cut, dark green leaves. It creates largish, full clumps and does well in partial shade, open filtered light, and even full sun. The seedpods are also interesting, looking like long beaks or "cranesbills."

MAINTENANCE AND REQUIREMENTS: The only downside to wild geranium is that the leaves tend to get flattened to the ground in heavy winds or rainstorms, but the beautiful blooms make up for that. Deadhead to prolong flowering and you'll have color for weeks.

PROPAGATION: Divide clumps in fall or early spring. If collecting seeds from the beaked "cranesbill"-like seed pod, you'll need to watch the plants carefully, as seeds are expelled as soon as they're ripe. (Or collect the pods as soon as they start to darken, and place in a paper bag; seeds will be expelled from the pod.)

GOOD COMPANIONS: A lovely combination for an open woodland planting is wild geranium with foamflower (*Tiarella cordifolia*), wild columbine (*Aquilegia canadensis*), Solomon's seal (*Polygonatum biflorum*), and goldenseal (*Hydrastis canadensis*). For a dramatic accent, plant a fire pink (*Silene virginica*) close to wild geranium.

RELATED SPECIES: In the northeast and midwest, try *G. bicknellii*, which has smaller flowers in a light shade of magenta. In the prairies and northwest, try *G. richardsonii*, a delicate and subtle plant with white flowers, purple veins, flowering in summer. A non-native relative, herb robert (*G. robertianum*), is quite invasive, especially in wild areas in the northwest.

MISCELLANY: The common non-native ornamental geranium is a *Pelargonium* and looks nothing like the native geranium.

WILD GINGER

Asarum canadense

HEIGHT: 6 inches (15 cm)
BLOOMING PERIOD: late spring
EXPOSURE: full to partial shade
MOISTURE: average to moist
HABITAT: woodlands
RANGE: northeast and prairies

DESCRIPTION: Wild ginger is an ideal groundcover for the woodland garden, as it spreads rapidly. Its leaves are large and heart-shaped, its stems hairy. A single flower (maroon, cup-shaped with three lobes) appears in late spring, close to the ground, hidden by the foliage.

MAINTENANCE AND REQUIREMENTS: Like so many woodlanders, wild ginger needs rich soil, full of organic material and moisture. If you provide these basic requirements, though, there's nothing else you need to do – this plant looks after itself. Prefers neutral to slightly acidic soil (pH 5.5 to 6.5) and is perfect for woodland rock gardens.

PROPAGATION: Divide the rhizomes in fall. Plant seed fresh, in early to mid-summer.

GOOD COMPANIONS: Wild ginger looks best when it has been given room to spread and when it's combined with something providing vertical interest, such as Solomon's seal (*Polygonatum biflorum*). A nice woodland combination includes fancy wood fern (*Dryopteris intermedia*), bloodroot (*Sanguinaria canadensis*), and false Solomon's seal (*Smilacina racemosa*).

RELATED SPECIES: The western species, *A. caudatum*, is evergreen and has shiny leaves; basic requirements and uses as above, though prefers acidic soil.

WILD LUPINE

Lupinus perennis

HEIGHT: 1–2 feet (30–60 cm)	**MOISTURE:** average to dry; drought tolerant
BLOOMING PERIOD: early summer	**HABITAT:** dry open woods, savannas
EXPOSURE: partial shade to full sun	**RANGE:** prairies and northeast

DESCRIPTION: Though the showy garden cultivars are nice, it would be great if more people sought the native species, as the wild lupine is the larval host plant for many butterflies in the blue family (including the endangered Karner blue). With typical palmate lupine leaves and tall elongated clusters of pea-like flowers, the wild lupine is a lovely addition to the garden and a perfect focal point in early summer. A legume, it fixes nitrogen in the soil.

MAINTENANCE AND REQUIREMENTS: Wild lupine requires good drainage, but other than that, is very versatile, growing in partial shade to full sun, slightly acidic to neutral soil, sand to heavier loam.

PROPAGATION: Start from seeds, which ripen in summer and should be sown fresh; scratch the hard seed coat to ensure germination. Ask at the nursery where seeds are purchased for the proper soil inoculant (which legumes require). Wild lupine does not transplant or divide well, due to its deep taproot, though it does self-sow.

GOOD COMPANIONS: Plant with butterfly weed (*Asclepias tuberosa*) and lance-leaved coreopsis (*Coreopsis lanceolata*).

RELATED SPECIES: In the northwest, try the large-leaved lupine (*L. polyphyllus*), which grows to 4 feet (1.2 m) in moist soil in partial shade to full sun and has large blue flowers.

WILDLIFE: Lupine is the larval host plant for the common blue butterfly, silvery blue butterfly, Karner blue, persius duskywing, afranius duskywing, and frosted elfin.

WILD QUININE

Parthenium integrifolium

HEIGHT: 2–3 feet (60–90 cm)
BLOOMING PERIOD: summer
EXPOSURE: full sun
MOISTURE: moist to dry; drought tolerant
HABITAT: prairies
RANGE: prairies

DESCRIPTION: It's only when you touch the flowers that you realize how strange they are: hard white little knobs. And the whole plant is as tough as it feels – covered in short, bristly hairs. This sturdy plant never flops over and is a fine addition to any prairie planting.

MAINTENANCE AND REQUIREMENTS: Wild quinine is an adaptable plant, growing in a wide range of conditions, from moist to dry soil, from sand to clay. All it needs is sun, though it can tolerate the open, filtered light of the woodland border.

PROPAGATION: Easy to start from seeds, which mature in early autumn.

GOOD COMPANIONS: A fine prairie combination includes false sunflower (*Heliopsis helianthoides*), lead-plant (*Amorpha canescens*), compass plant (*Silphium laciniatum*), rattlesnake master (*Eryngium yuccifolium*), purple coneflower (*Echinacea purpurea*), and wild bergamot (*Monarda fistulosa*).

This prairie combination includes blue vervain (*Verbena hastata*), swamp milkweed (*Asclepias incarnata*), evening primrose (*Oenothera biennis*), and purple coneflower (*Echinacea purpurea*). The same species could be used to create a more formal design, but in this wonderful wild garden they mimic the look of nature.

WILD SENNA

Cassia hebecarpa

HEIGHT: 3–6 feet (.9–1.8 m)
BLOOMING PERIOD: summer
EXPOSURE: full sun to light shade
MOISTURE: moist to average
HABITAT: meadows
RANGE: prairies and northeast

DESCRIPTION: As you know by now, I love most leguminous plants, especially for their leaves and pea-like flowers – and I'm enthusiastic in my promotion of them. There, my bias is on the table. Wild senna has those wonderfully characteristic pinnately compound leaves and branched clusters of yellow flowers throughout the latter half of the summer. It gets quite bushy, almost appearing to be a shrub, and can get floppy.

MAINTENANCE AND REQUIREMENTS: Wild senna is easy to care for – give it moist to average soil, in full sun to light shade, sand to heavier loam, neutral pH, and it will thrive.

PROPAGATION: Easy to start from seeds, which mature in early fall, or by dividing the plant in early spring or in fall.

GOOD COMPANIONS: Grow wild senna with purple coneflower (*Echinacea purpurea*), panic grass (*Panicum virgatum*), New Jersey tea (*Ceanothus americanus*), and wild bergamot (*Monarda fistulosa*). In a moist site, combine with New England aster (*Aster novae-angliae*).

RELATED SPECIES: Partridge pea (*C. fasciculata*) has larger flowers and grows 1 to 2 feet (30 to 60 cm), preferring sandy soil.

WILDLIFE: Larval host plant for the cloudless sulphur butterfly. Attracts hummingbirds.

WOOD POPPY

Stylophorum diphyllum

HEIGHT: 1–1½ feet (30–45 cm)	**MOISTURE:** average to moist
BLOOMING PERIOD: spring	**HABITAT:** rich woods
EXPOSURE: shade to partial shade	**RANGE:** prairies and northeast

DESCRIPTION: One look at the wood poppy demolishes the myth that color is hard to come by in the shade garden. In spring, the plant is covered with yellow blooms that light up any dim corner. Growing into a full, nicely bushy but not tall plant, wood poppy has irregularly lobed leaves that range in color from light to dark green. I replaced a clump of daffodils with wood poppy and couldn't be happier with the result – no dying bulb foliage to deal with.

MAINTENANCE AND REQUIREMENTS: You'll have more success with wood poppy if your woodland soil is on the moist side throughout the summer. During periods of drought, the leaves may wither or turn yellow. Mulch well to retain moisture and regenerate the soil with well-rotted compost. Wood poppy readily self-sows.

PROPAGATION: If starting from seeds, plant fresh and don't let them dry out. Easy to increase through division in spring or fall.

GOOD COMPANIONS: A spring show of spectacular color includes wood poppy, wild phlox (*Phlox divaricata*), white trillium (*Trillium grandiflorum*), twinleaf (*Jeffersonia diphylla*), Virginia bluebells (*Mertensia virginica*), and false Solomon's seal (*Smilacina racemosa*). Wood poppy also looks good with lacy ferns such as male fern (*Dryopteris filix-mas*) and New York fern (*Thelypteris noveboracensis*), and with foamflower (*Tiarella cordifolia*).

MISCELLANY: Although sometimes called celandine poppy, don't confuse it with the non-native (and invasive) celandine (*Chelidonium majus*), which looks quite similar but behaves much more aggressively.

WOOD SORREL

Oxalis oregana

HEIGHT: 8 inches (20 cm)
BLOOMING PERIOD: spring through summer
EXPOSURE: partial shade to deep shade
MOISTURE: moist to average
HABITAT: moist conifer forests
RANGE: northwest

DESCRIPTION: Nothing creates as cool and inviting a woodland retreat as a carpet of wood sorrel. Its clover-like leaves are stunning (a rich green) and ever-changing (they fold up at night or when soil dries out or in response to rain; they droop in sunlight). Single flowers are small and white or pinkish (with reddish to purple veins) in spring; stems are hairy. Wonderful as a groundcover in deep shade.

MAINTENANCE AND REQUIREMENTS: Wood sorrel does best and spreads most quickly (by creeping rhizomes) in rich, moist, acidic to slightly neutral soil in shade. But give it a try in regular soils too, in shade, as it will grow but not spread as quickly.

PROPAGATION: Divide rhizomes in early spring. Seeds appear throughout the summer; plant fresh.

GOOD COMPANIONS: For a nice contrast of foliage shapes, plant with deer fern (*Blechnum spicant*) – the wood sorrel will carpet the ground and deer fern will send up its perky fronds. False Solomon's seal (*Smilacina racemosa*) is also a good companion, as are western bleeding heart (*Dicentra formosa*) and western trillium (*Trillium ovatum*).

RELATED SPECIES: Western yellow oxalis (*O. suksdorfii*) has yellow flowers. In the prairies, try violet wood sorrel (*O. violacea*), which has rose-purple flowers, or yellow wood sorrel (*O. stricta*), which has small yellow flowers in late summer.

YELLOW CONEFLOWER

Ratibida pinnata

HEIGHT: 3–5 feet (90–150 cm)	**MOISTURE:** average to dry; drought tolerant
BLOOMING PERIOD: mid- to late summer	**HABITAT:** prairies, meadows
EXPOSURE: full sun to partial sun	**RANGE:** prairies and northeast

DESCRIPTION: A signature plant of the prairies, yellow coneflower is perfect for sunny meadow or prairie gardens. (The only downside is that it can get floppy if not supported by other plants.) Its flowers are prolific, long-lasting, and a luminous yellow; the petals (ray flowers) droop and the brownish cone in the center sticks up. Leaves are divided into coarsely toothed segments.

MAINTENANCE AND REQUIREMENTS: Tolerant of a wide range of soils, from sandy to clayey, yellow coneflower is very easy to grow. It prefers full sun but I've seen it doing well in partial sun. Its stems often aren't very strong, so give it support.

PROPAGATION: Easy to start from seeds, which mature in mid-autumn, or by dividing clumps.

GOOD COMPANIONS: There are always lots of yellows in the prairie garden, so I'd suggest some purples and blues for contrast: for example, purple coneflower (*Echinacea purpurea*) and western ironweed (*Vernonia fasciculata*).

RELATED SPECIES: Prairie coneflower (*R. columnifera*) has a taller (sillier-looking) central disk, but the whole plant is shorter, 2 to 3 feet (60 to 90 cm).

WILDLIFE: Attracts birds and butterflies.

MISCELLANY: Also known as gray-headed coneflower.

ZIG ZAG GOLDENROD

Solidago flexicaulis

HEIGHT: 1–3 feet (30–90 cm)
BLOOMING PERIOD: late summer to fall
EXPOSURE: full shade to filtered light
MOISTURE: average to dry
HABITAT: woodlands
RANGE: prairies and northeast

DESCRIPTION: A garden-saver in dry shade, zig zag goldenrod gets its name from its zig-zag, angled stem, which is an interesting feature. Its flowers are wonderful yellow blasts of color in the late-summer woodland.

MAINTENANCE AND REQUIREMENTS: Zig zag goldenrod is not particularly needy with regard to nutrients and organic matter – it's unusual for a woodland plant in this way. It doesn't need mulching, either, both because it's adapted to dry conditions and because it will outcompete most weeds (two common reasons to mulch).

PROPAGATION: You can start zig zag goldenrod from seeds, which mature in late autumn, but you can also just leave it to spread on its own.

GOOD COMPANIONS: There's not much blooming in the woodland garden in late summer, so include a mass of zig zag goldenrod for some late-summer color and to brighten up a foliage corner. For a nice foliage contrast, plant with spikenard (*Aralia racemosa*).

RELATED SPECIES: In sunny conditions, one of my favorite goldenrods is the grass-leaved goldenrod (*S. graminifolia*): it gets quite bushy, almost like a tall shrub (1 to 4 feet/30 to 120 cm), with very fine willow-like leaves, and in mid-summer through to fall, it is covered with small yellow flowers. It's a fragrant cloud of color and I highly recommend it, though it is highly invasive. See also the entry for stiff goldenrod (S. *rigida*).

ETHICAL GARDENER'S GUIDELINES

1 Do not disrupt native plant communities.

2 Obtain native plants from seed, garden, or nursery.

3 Buy only wildflowers and ferns certified by the vendors as: "Nursery Propagated."

4 Use plants and seeds which have originated in your immediate bioregion. Such plants and seeds are best adapted to the local climate, soil, predators, pollinators, and disease.

5 Give preference to bioregionally native plant species in your garden, rather than naturalized or exotic species. The latter group may escape to wild habitats and interfere with the growth and spread of native flora and fauna.

6 Promote the cultivation and propagation of bioregionally native plants as an educational and conservation measure to supplement the preservation of natural habitat.

7 Keep accurate records of any bioregionally rare flora which you are growing to increase our understanding of the biology of the species.

8 Transplant wild native flora only when the plants of a given area are officially slated for destruction: e.g., road construction, subdivisions, pipelines, golf courses, etc. Obtain permission before transplanting.

9 Collect no more than 10 percent of a seed crop from the wild. Leave the rest for natural dispersal and as food for dependent organisms.

10 Use natural means of fertilizing, weed, and predator control rather than synthetic chemical means.

11 Consider planting native species attractive to native fauna, especially birds, butterflies, and moths uncommon to your bioregion.

12 Exercise extreme caution when studying and photographing wildflowers in order not to damage the surrounding flora and fauna.

13 Co-operate with institutions such as arboreta, botanical gardens, museums, and universities in the propagation and study of rare species.

14 Openly share your botanical knowledge with the public but ensure that native plant species or communities will not be damaged in the process.

(Reprinted with permission from the North American Native Plant Society.)

PROPAGATION

When I first started gardening, I grew non-native species and spring was the time to plant seeds. As I gradually learned more about native plants, it took me the longest time to switch gears and realize that many native seeds are best planted in the autumn. For someone familiar with conventional gardening methods, it seemed counter-intuitive to plant seeds just as winter was about to arrive. Actually, though, it makes perfect sense.

In the native plant garden, nature is model and guide, and in the wild, the seeds of many species ripen, then go through a long season of cold dormancy – winter – before germinating. The easiest thing to do is to mimic the process, potting up seeds in the autumn and leaving them outdoors for the winter (covered, if necessary, to protect them from predation). The seeds of many natives require this cold period before they'll break dormancy and sprout.

However, there are some natives, such as columbine, that don't require a cold period and I've noted this in the listings. These seeds can be planted as soon as they ripen, or the next spring.

Some of us (myself included) aren't organized enough to pot up seeds in fall, or we're given seeds in very early spring. In these situations, we need to fake the seeds' cold dormancy period. It's a process called seed stratification, basically a fancy name for sticking seeds in the fridge for a few weeks. Put seeds in a plastic pouch or paper bag, label them, and leave them in the fridge for six to eight weeks prior to planting in spring. This make-like-winter trick will work for the majority of plants listed in this book.

The exceptions are ferns (see separate section that follows) and a few natives that require not only cold stratification but cold *moist* stratification. For these species, which are noted in the listings, put seeds with some damp sand or damp peat moss in an airtight container in the fridge. Or, of course, you can just plant them outside in autumn – nature will do the required cold moist stratification for you.

Some seeds, such as Jack-in-the-pulpit and trout lily, should always be sown fresh, as soon as they ripen, rather than being allowed to dry out. Plants with this requirement are noted in the listings. As for how to tell that seeds are ripe or mature, there are some general guidelines, though nothing beats observation and trial and error. Watch seed pods or berries and see if they start to expand or turn darker in color – two sure signs of maturation. In general, seeds mature approximately four to six weeks after flowering.

If all this sounds like high science or far too

much to remember, rest assured that all you really need to do is think about what happens in the wild. If a seed matures in late summer or fall, chances are that it requires the cold stratification nature provides (or, at least, that it won't be harmed by cold stratification). If a plant's seeds are contained in a fleshy berry, chances are it should be planted fresh, and the seed not allowed to dry out prior to planting.

Starting plants from seed does take patience. If you're looking for a faster method of propagation, consider division. For best results, divide spring-blooming plants in the fall and fall-blooming plants in the spring. Simply dig out the mature plant, shake the soil loose, and tease or cut apart (you may need to use a trowel or knife). Replant immediately and water well.

Root cuttings can also be taken when a plant is dormant. Cut 2- to 4-inch (5 to 10 cm) sections from a large ($1/4$ to $1/2$ inch/.25 to .5 cm in diameter) root, ensuring that each cutting has a couple of buds (small bumps) and place horizontally in potting soil. Cover with 1 inch (2.5 cm) of soil and water.

Rhizome cuttings are similar to root cuttings (rhizomes are underground stems) and should also be taken when the plant is dormant. Dig around the plant to locate rhizomes (they look like thick roots), sever the rhizome from the parent plant, and cut it into 3-inch (7.5 cm) sections, each of which should have a few buds. Plant horizontally, cover with soil, and water.

PROPAGATING FERNS

Until I took a day-long fern course at the Guelph Arboretum in Ontario, I thought fern propagation was a deep dark secret – something to do with mysterious, prehistoric plant parts called sporangia – best left to experts. But it's actually very simple. Ferns reproduce via spores, which are encased in sporangia that look like tiny black dots on the undersides of fronds. These sporangia appear at different times on different fern species, and the spores inside the cases mature at different rates. You can use a magnifying glass to see if the spore case is opening up, which signals maturity, or you can just remove a fertile frond and place it on a sheet of paper (inside, where there's no wind). Within a few hours to a day, you'll notice thousands of tiny spores dotting the paper.

Take a clear plastic container that has a lid (like the ones danishes come in), fill it with a sterile mix of sand, potting soil, and peat moss, and sprinkle the spores over the surface. Mist with a spray bottle, close the lid, and put the container in a warm, bright spot out of direct sun. After a few days, you'll notice strange green growths (called prothalli) on the surface. Mist regularly (every few days) after the prothalli appear, keeping the lid closed afterwards, and in a few weeks to a few months, the prothalli will develop into tiny young ferns. You may need to thin them, but don't transplant them into larger pots until they have three or four fronds each.

PLANTS FOR SPECIFIC CONDITIONS: QUICK-REFERENCE CHARTS

The following charts indicate native plants that are appropriate for specific conditions, such as acidic soil, or particular locations, such as the northwest region. Use the charts for handy reference (and inspiration), and then read the full listing to make sure that the plant meets all your requirements.

Plants for Woodland Habitat
Plants for Meadow Habitat
Plants for Prairie Habitat
Plants for Northwest Region
Plants for Prairie Region
Plants for Northeast Region
Drought-Tolerant Plants
Plants that Tolerate Dry Soil in Shade or Partial Shade
Plants for Acidic Soil
Plants for Deep Shade
Plants for Moist Areas
Plants that Attract Butterflies

PLANTS FOR WOODLAND HABITAT

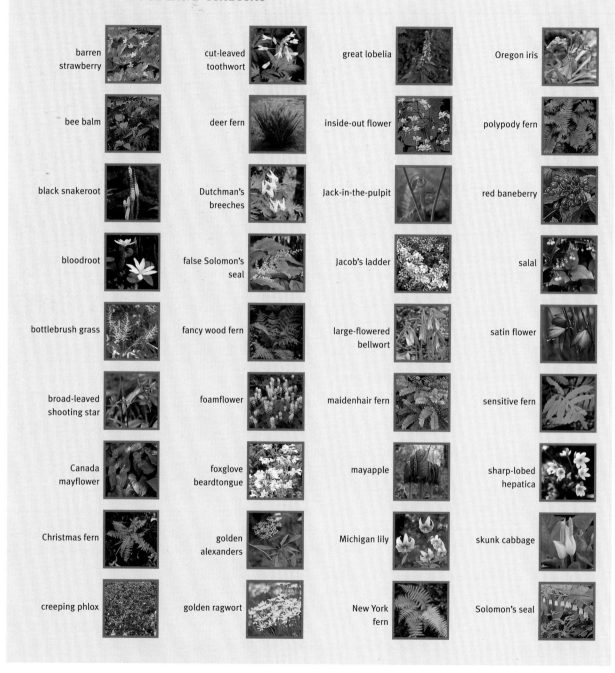

barren strawberry	cut-leaved toothwort	great lobelia	Oregon iris
bee balm	deer fern	inside-out flower	polypody fern
black snakeroot	Dutchman's breeches	Jack-in-the-pulpit	red baneberry
bloodroot	false Solomon's seal	Jacob's ladder	salal
bottlebrush grass	fancy wood fern	large-flowered bellwort	satin flower
broad-leaved shooting star	foamflower	maidenhair fern	sensitive fern
Canada mayflower	foxglove beardtongue	mayapple	sharp-lobed hepatica
Christmas fern	golden alexanders	Michigan lily	skunk cabbage
creeping phlox	golden ragwort	New York fern	Solomon's seal

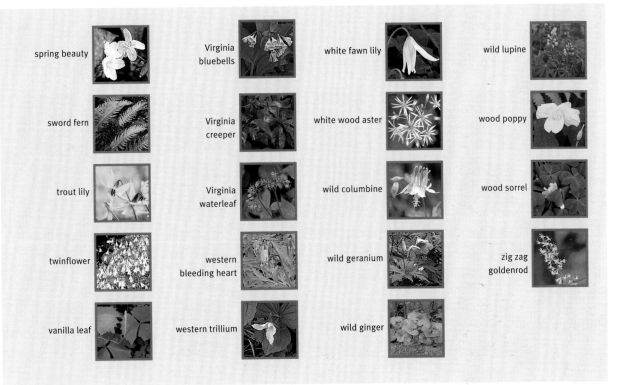

spring beauty

Virginia bluebells

white fawn lily

wild lupine

sword fern

Virginia creeper

white wood aster

wood poppy

trout lily

Virginia waterleaf

wild columbine

wood sorrel

twinflower

western bleeding heart

wild geranium

zig zag goldenrod

vanilla leaf

western trillium

wild ginger

PLANTS FOR MEADOW HABITAT

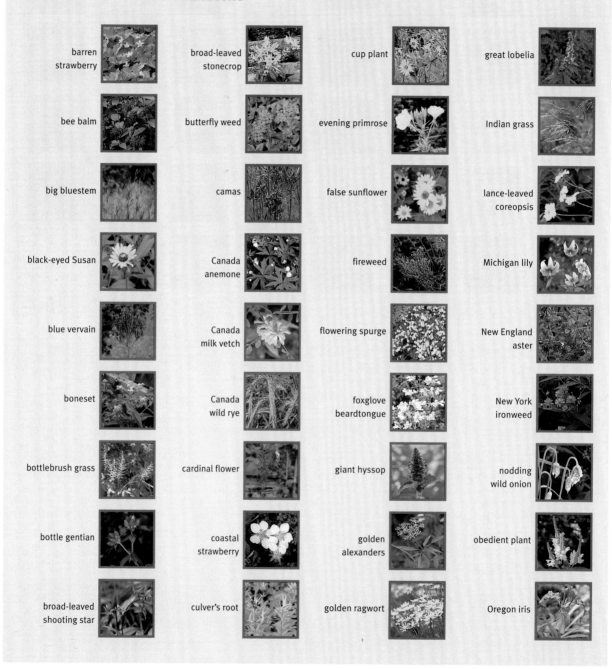

barren strawberry	broad-leaved stonecrop	cup plant	great lobelia
bee balm	butterfly weed	evening primrose	Indian grass
big bluestem	camas	false sunflower	lance-leaved coreopsis
black-eyed Susan	Canada anemone	fireweed	Michigan lily
blue vervain	Canada milk vetch	flowering spurge	New England aster
boneset	Canada wild rye	foxglove beardtongue	New York ironweed
bottlebrush grass	cardinal flower	giant hyssop	nodding wild onion
bottle gentian	coastal strawberry	golden alexanders	obedient plant
broad-leaved shooting star	culver's root	golden ragwort	Oregon iris

Oregon sunshine

rough blazing star

spotted Joe-pye weed

wild bergamot

pasque flower

satin flower

stiff goldenrod

wild columbine

purple coneflower

sensitive fern

swamp milkweed

wild lupine

Queen of the prairie

showy tick trefoil

virgin's bower

wild senna

rattlesnake master

spiderwort

white fawn lily

yellow coneflower

PLANTS FOR PRAIRIE HABITAT

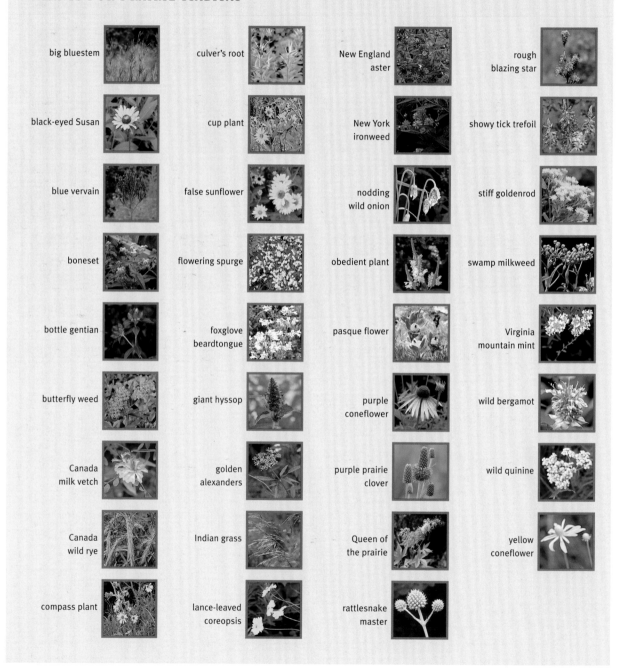

big bluestem	culver's root	New England aster	rough blazing star
black-eyed Susan	cup plant	New York ironweed	showy tick trefoil
blue vervain	false sunflower	nodding wild onion	stiff goldenrod
boneset	flowering spurge	obedient plant	swamp milkweed
bottle gentian	foxglove beardtongue	pasque flower	Virginia mountain mint
butterfly weed	giant hyssop	purple coneflower	wild bergamot
Canada milk vetch	golden alexanders	purple prairie clover	wild quinine
Canada wild rye	Indian grass	Queen of the prairie	yellow coneflower
compass plant	lance-leaved coreopsis	rattlesnake master	

PLANTS FOR NORTHWEST REGION

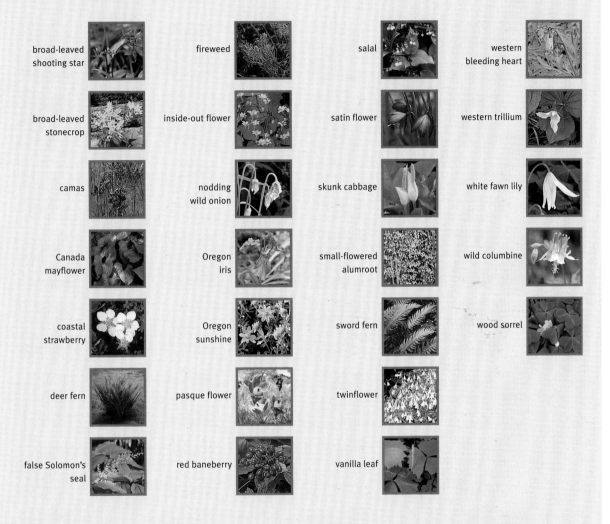

broad-leaved shooting star

broad-leaved stonecrop

camas

Canada mayflower

coastal strawberry

deer fern

false Solomon's seal

fireweed

inside-out flower

nodding wild onion

Oregon iris

Oregon sunshine

pasque flower

red baneberry

salal

satin flower

skunk cabbage

small-flowered alumroot

sword fern

twinflower

vanilla leaf

western bleeding heart

western trillium

white fawn lily

wild columbine

wood sorrel

NOTE: The plants covered in this book are evenly divided between northwest, prairie, and northeast species. However, you'll notice from the following three reference charts, divided into regions, that there appear to be more northeast and prairie species than northwest species. This is due to the fact that a number of the prairie species have ranges that extend *partially* into the northeast; likewise, some of the northeast species extend *partially* into the prairie region. Thus, these species appear on both lists, bumping up the numbers. On the other hand, most of the northwest species do not extend into the prairies or northeast, so they are listed only on the northwest quick reference chart.

Plants For Prairie Region

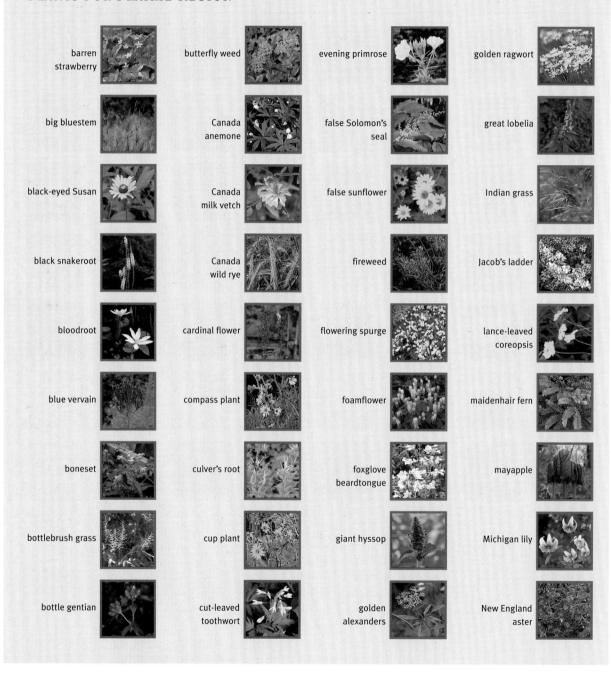

barren strawberry	butterfly weed	evening primrose	golden ragwort
big bluestem	Canada anemone	false Solomon's seal	great lobelia
black-eyed Susan	Canada milk vetch	false sunflower	Indian grass
black snakeroot	Canada wild rye	fireweed	Jacob's ladder
bloodroot	cardinal flower	flowering spurge	lance-leaved coreopsis
blue vervain	compass plant	foamflower	maidenhair fern
boneset	culver's root	foxglove beardtongue	mayapple
bottlebrush grass	cup plant	giant hyssop	Michigan lily
bottle gentian	cut-leaved toothwort	golden alexanders	New England aster

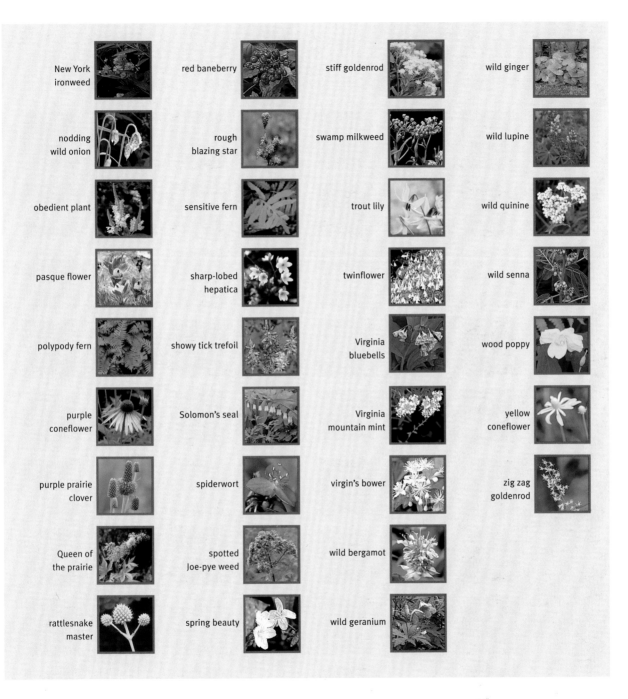

New York
ironweed

red baneberry

stiff goldenrod

wild ginger

nodding
wild onion

rough
blazing star

swamp milkweed

wild lupine

obedient plant

sensitive fern

trout lily

wild quinine

pasque flower

sharp-lobed
hepatica

twinflower

wild senna

polypody fern

showy tick trefoil

Virginia
bluebells

wood poppy

purple
coneflower

Solomon's seal

Virginia
mountain mint

yellow
coneflower

purple prairie
clover

spiderwort

virgin's bower

zig zag
goldenrod

Queen of
the prairie

spotted
Joe-pye weed

wild bergamot

rattlesnake
master

spring beauty

wild geranium

PLANTS FOR NORTHEAST REGION

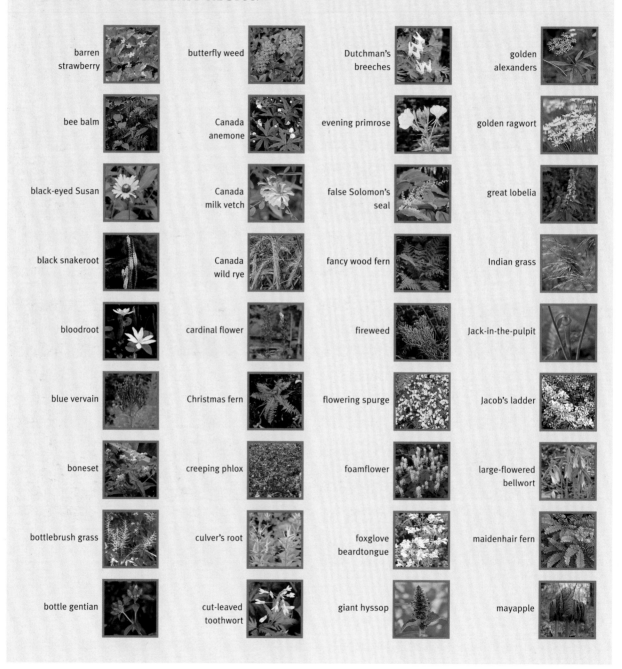

barren strawberry

butterfly weed

Dutchman's breeches

golden alexanders

bee balm

Canada anemone

evening primrose

golden ragwort

black-eyed Susan

Canada milk vetch

false Solomon's seal

great lobelia

black snakeroot

Canada wild rye

fancy wood fern

Indian grass

bloodroot

cardinal flower

fireweed

Jack-in-the-pulpit

blue vervain

Christmas fern

flowering spurge

Jacob's ladder

boneset

creeping phlox

foamflower

large-flowered bellwort

bottlebrush grass

culver's root

foxglove beardtongue

maidenhair fern

bottle gentian

cut-leaved toothwort

giant hyssop

mayapple

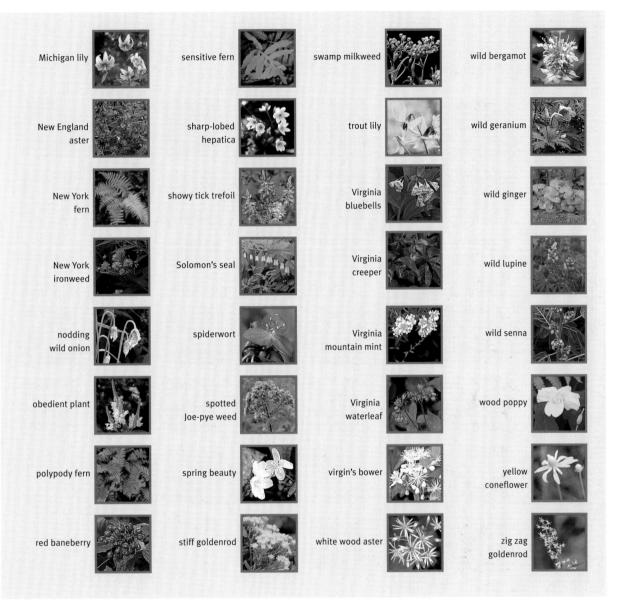

Michigan lily

New England aster

New York fern

New York ironweed

nodding wild onion

obedient plant

polypody fern

red baneberry

sensitive fern

sharp-lobed hepatica

showy tick trefoil

Solomon's seal

spiderwort

spotted Joe-pye weed

spring beauty

stiff goldenrod

swamp milkweed

trout lily

Virginia bluebells

Virginia creeper

Virginia mountain mint

Virginia waterleaf

virgin's bower

white wood aster

wild bergamot

wild geranium

wild ginger

wild lupine

wild senna

wood poppy

yellow coneflower

zig zag goldenrod

DROUGHT-TOLERANT PLANTS

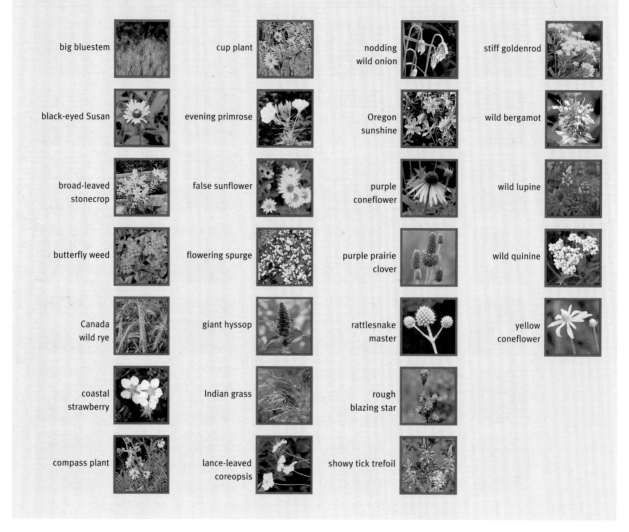

big bluestem

black-eyed Susan

broad-leaved stonecrop

butterfly weed

Canada wild rye

coastal strawberry

compass plant

cup plant

evening primrose

false sunflower

flowering spurge

giant hyssop

Indian grass

lance-leaved coreopsis

nodding wild onion

Oregon sunshine

purple coneflower

purple prairie clover

rattlesnake master

rough blazing star

showy tick trefoil

stiff goldenrod

wild bergamot

wild lupine

wild quinine

yellow coneflower

PLANTS THAT TOLERATE DRY SOIL IN SHADE OR PARTIAL SHADE

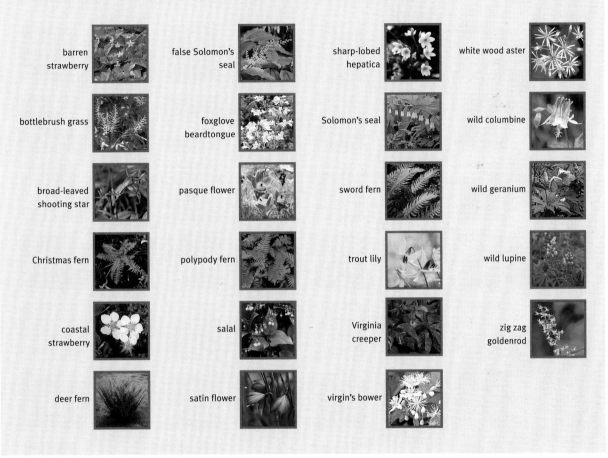

barren strawberry

false Solomon's seal

sharp-lobed hepatica

white wood aster

bottlebrush grass

foxglove beardtongue

Solomon's seal

wild columbine

broad-leaved shooting star

pasque flower

sword fern

wild geranium

Christmas fern

polypody fern

trout lily

wild lupine

coastal strawberry

salal

Virginia creeper

zig zag goldenrod

deer fern

satin flower

virgin's bower

PLANTS FOR ACIDIC SOIL

black-eyed Susan	culver's root	New York ironweed	swamp milkweed
black snakeroot	deer fern	nodding wild onion	sword fern
bottle gentian	false Solomon's seal	polypody fern	twinflower
broad-leaved stonecrop	foamflower	purple coneflower	vanilla leaf
camas	golden alexanders	rough blazing star	western bleeding heart
Canada mayflower	inside-out flower	salal	western trillium
cardinal flower	Jack-in-the-pulpit	skunk cabbage	white fawn lily
Christmas fern	New England aster	Solomon's seal	wild columbine
coastal strawberry	New York fern	spring beauty	wood sorrel

PLANTS FOR DEEP SHADE

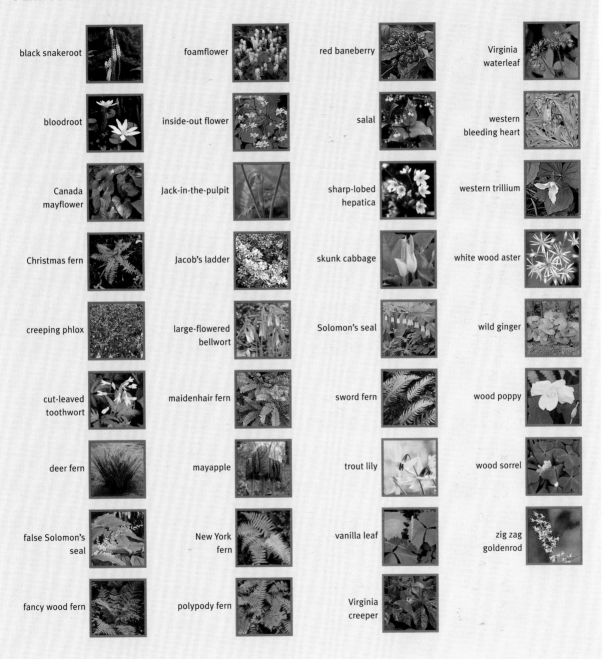

black snakeroot

bloodroot

Canada mayflower

Christmas fern

creeping phlox

cut-leaved toothwort

deer fern

false Solomon's seal

fancy wood fern

foamflower

inside-out flower

Jack-in-the-pulpit

Jacob's ladder

large-flowered bellwort

maidenhair fern

mayapple

New York fern

polypody fern

red baneberry

salal

sharp-lobed hepatica

skunk cabbage

Solomon's seal

sword fern

trout lily

vanilla leaf

Virginia creeper

Virginia waterleaf

western bleeding heart

western trillium

white wood aster

wild ginger

wood poppy

wood sorrel

zig zag goldenrod

Plants For Moist Areas

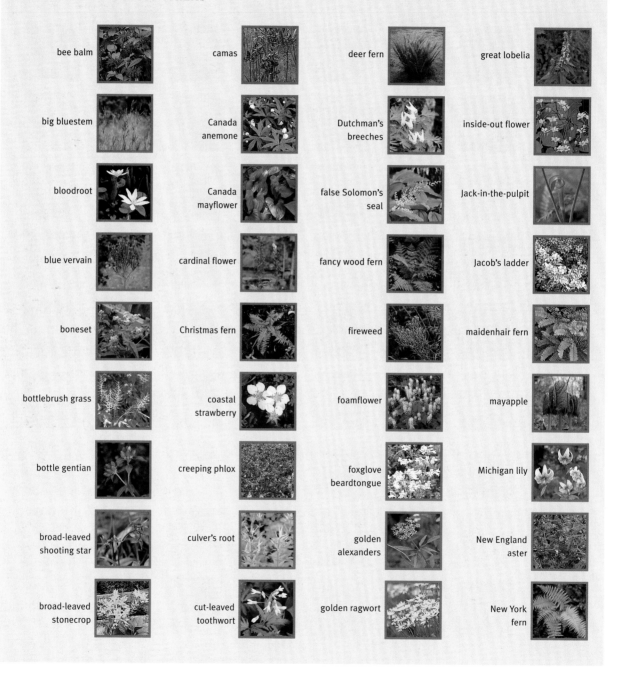

bee balm	camas	deer fern	great lobelia
big bluestem	Canada anemone	Dutchman's breeches	inside-out flower
bloodroot	Canada mayflower	false Solomon's seal	Jack-in-the-pulpit
blue vervain	cardinal flower	fancy wood fern	Jacob's ladder
boneset	Christmas fern	fireweed	maidenhair fern
bottlebrush grass	coastal strawberry	foamflower	mayapple
bottle gentian	creeping phlox	foxglove beardtongue	Michigan lily
broad-leaved shooting star	culver's root	golden alexanders	New England aster
broad-leaved stonecrop	cut-leaved toothwort	golden ragwort	New York fern

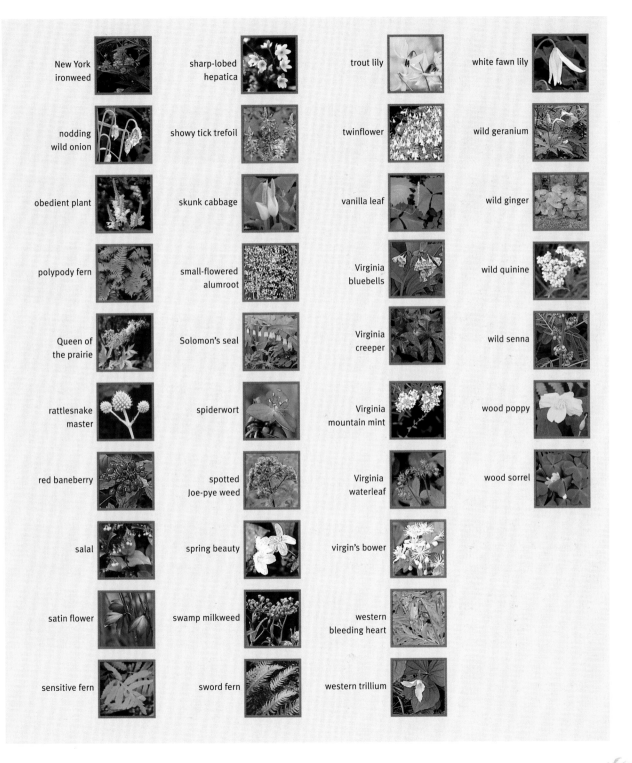

New York ironweed

sharp-lobed hepatica

trout lily

white fawn lily

nodding wild onion

showy tick trefoil

twinflower

wild geranium

obedient plant

skunk cabbage

vanilla leaf

wild ginger

polypody fern

small-flowered alumroot

Virginia bluebells

wild quinine

Queen of the prairie

Solomon's seal

Virginia creeper

wild senna

rattlesnake master

spiderwort

Virginia mountain mint

wood poppy

red baneberry

spotted Joe-pye weed

Virginia waterleaf

wood sorrel

salal

spring beauty

virgin's bower

satin flower

swamp milkweed

western bleeding heart

sensitive fern

sword fern

western trillium

PLANTS THAT ATTRACT BUTTERFLIES

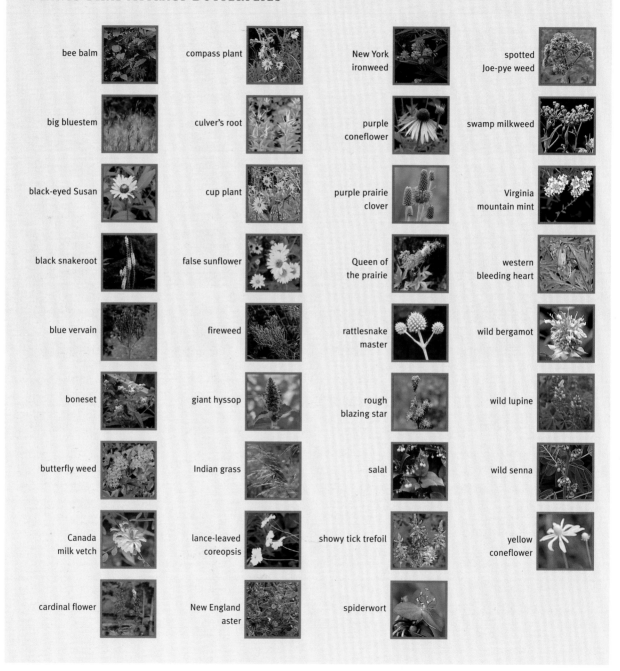

bee balm

big bluestem

black-eyed Susan

black snakeroot

blue vervain

boneset

butterfly weed

Canada milk vetch

cardinal flower

compass plant

culver's root

cup plant

false sunflower

fireweed

giant hyssop

Indian grass

lance-leaved coreopsis

New England aster

New York ironweed

purple coneflower

purple prairie clover

Queen of the prairie

rattlesnake master

rough blazing star

salal

showy tick trefoil

spiderwort

spotted Joe-pye weed

swamp milkweed

Virginia mountain mint

western bleeding heart

wild bergamot

wild lupine

wild senna

yellow coneflower

A SELECTION OF NORTH AMERICAN NATIVE PLANT NURSERIES

NORTHWEST REGION

A'Qam Native Plant Nursery
c/o Ktunaxa Kinbasket Treaty
  Council
7468 Mission Road
Cranbrook, British Columbia
  V1C 7E5
aqam@rockies.net

B.C.'s Wild Heritage Plants
47330 Extrom Road
Chilliwack, British Columbia
  V2R 4V1
(604) 858-5141
bcwild@uniserve.com

Bosky Dell Natives
23311 SW Bosky Dell Lane
West Linn, Oregon 97068-9130
(503) 638-5945
www.boskydellnatives.com

Burnt Ridge Nursery
432 Burnt Ridge Road
Onalaska, Washington 98570
(360) 985-2873
http://landru.myhome.net/
burntridge

Dry Valley Nurseries
667 Curtis Road
Kelowna, British Columbia
  V1V 2C9
(250) 860-6468
www.dryvalleynurseries.com

Fraser's Thimble Farms
175 Arbutus Road
Salt Spring Island, British
  Columbia V8K 1A3
(250) 537-5788
www.thimblefarms.com

Frosty Hollow Ecological
  Restoration
P.O. Box 53
Langley, Washington 98260
(360) 579-2332
wean@whidbey.net

Inside Passage
P.O. Box 639
Port Townsend, Washington
  98368-0639
(360) 385-6114
www.insidepassageseeds.com

MSK Rare Plant Nursery
20066–15th Avenue
Seattle, Washington 98177
(206) 546-1281

Maxwelton Valley Gardens
3443 E. French Road
Clinton, Washington 98236
(360) 579-1770
www.whidbey.net/mvg/

Natives Northwest
190 Aldrich Road
Mossyrock, Washington
  98564-9609
(360) 983-3138
aldrich@myhome.net

Natural Habitat Gardens
R.R. 1, S15A, C35
Sorrento, British Columbia
  V0E 2W0
(250) 835-2221
www3.telus.net/public/a5a43197

Natural Resource Native Plant
  Nursery
2466 Roome Road
Duncan, British Columbia
  V9L 4L2
(250) 748-0684
www.oud-naturalresource.com

Pacific Rim Native Plant Nursery
44305 Old Orchard Road
Chilliwack, British Columbia
  V2R 1A9
(604) 792-9279
www.hillkeep.ca

Peel's Nurseries Ltd.
11610 Sylvester Road
Mission, British Columbia
  V2V 4J1
(604) 820-7381
www.peelsnurseries.com

Sagebrush Native Plant Nursery
38206 93rd Street, R.R. 2, Site
  13, Comp. 10
Oliver, British Columbia
  V0H 1T0
(250) 498-8898

Sound Native Plants
P.O. Box 7505
Olympia, Washington
  98507-7505
(360) 352-4122
www.soundnativeplants.com

Streamside Native Plants
3222 Grant Road
Courtenay, British Columbia
  V9J 1L2
(250) 338-7509
www.streamsidenativeplants.
com

Wildside Native Plant Nursery
1770 Corrigal Road
Denman Island, British
  Columbia V0R 1T0
(250) 335-1379
wildside@island.net

Woodgate Native Plant Services
2558 Jackson Valley Road
Box 508
Duncan, British Columbia
  V9C 3X8
(250) 748-2558
www.natplants.nbm.ca

PRAIRIE REGION

ALCLA Native Plant Restoration
    Inc.
3208 Bearspaw Drive Northwest
Calgary, Alberta T2L 1T2
(403) 282-6516
www.ALCLAnativeplants.com

Alberta Nurseries & Seeds Ltd.
Box 20
Bowden, Alberta T0M 0K0
(403) 224-3545
www.marketland.net

Blazing Star Wild Flower
    Seed Co.
General Delivery
Didsbury, Alberta T0M 0W0
(403) 335-4956
http://growwildflowers.com

Bluestem Farm
S5920 Lehman Road
Baraboo, Wisconsin 53913
(608) 356-0179
www.bluestemfarm.com

EnviroScapes
Box 38
Warner, Alberta T0K 2L0
(403) 733-2160
enscapes@telusplanet.net

Prairie Garden Seeds
Box 118
Cochin, Saskatchewan S0M 0L0
(306) 386-2737
www.prseeds.ca

Prairie Habitats
P.O. Box 1
Argyle, Manitoba R0C 0B0
(204) 467-9371
www.prairiehabitats.com

Prairie Moon Nursery
31837 Bur Oak Lane
Winona, Minnesota 55987
(507) 452-1362
www.prairiemoon.com

Prairie Nursery
P.O. Box 306
Westfield, Wisconsin
    53964-0116
(608) 296-3679
www.prairienursery.com

Prairie Originals
17 Schreyer Crescent
St. Andrews, Manitoba R1A 3A6
(204) 338-7517
prairieo@mts.net

Prairie Ridge Nursery
9738 Overland Road
Mt. Horeb, Wisconsin
    53572-2832
(608) 437-5245
www.prairieridgenursery.com

Prairie Seeds
1805-8th Street
Nisku, Alberta T9E 7S8
(780) 955-7345
www.prairieseeds.com

Prairiescape
2080 Athol Street
Regina, Saskatchewan S4T 3E5
(306) 352-2266

Taylor Creek Restoration
    Nurseries
17921 Smith Road
Brodhead, Wisconsin 53520
(608) 897-8641
www.appliedeco.com

NORTHEAST REGION

Acorus Restoration
722 6th Concession Road, R.R. 1
Walsingham, Ontario N0E 1X0
(519) 586-2603
www.ecologyart.com

Appalachian Wildflower Nursery
Route 1, Box 275A
Reedsville, Pennsylvania 17084
(717) 667-6998

Environmental Concern Inc.
P.O. Box P
St. Michaels, Maryland 21663
(410) 745-9620
www.wetland.org

Gardens North
5984 Third Line Road North
North Gower, Ontario K0A 2T0
(613) 489-0065
www.gardensnorth.com

Grand Moraine Growers
7369 12th Line, R.R. 2
Alma, Ontario N0B 1A0
(519) 638-1101
www.sentex.net/~pems/

Indigo
80 Route 116
Ulverton, Quebec J0B 2B0
www.horticulture-indigo.com

MacPhail Woods
R.R. 3
Belfast, Prince Edward Island
    C1A 1H9
(902) 651-2575
www.macphailwoods.org

Murray's Horticultural Services
    Ltd.
Box 182
Portugal Cove, Newfoundland
    A0A 3K0
(709) 895-2800

New England Wild Flower
    Society
180 Hemenway Road
Framingham, Massachusetts
    01701-2699
(508) 877-7630
www.newfs.org

Oka Fleurs Nursery
1945 Chemin Oka, C.P. 524
Oka, Quebec J0N 1E0
(514) 479-6963

Old Field Garden and
    Wildflower Nursery
2935 Porter Road, R.R. 1
Oxford Station, Ontario K0G 1T0
(613) 258-7924
www.oldfieldgarden.on.ca

Orford Moraine Restoration
14738 McDonald Line, R.R. 1
Muirkirk, Ontario N0L 1X0
(519) 678-3866
www.carolinianplants.com

Otter Valley Native Plants
Box 31, R.R. 1
Eden, Ontario N0J 1H0
(519) 866-5639
otter.va@amtelecom.net

Pterophylla
R.R. 1
Walsingham, Ontario N0E 1X0
(519) 586-3985
gartcar@kwic.com

Sweet Grass Gardens
Six Nations of the Grand River
R.R. 6
Hagersville, Ontario N0A 1H0
(519) 445-4828
www.sweetgrassgardens.com

WILD Canada
75 39th Street North
Wasaga Beach, Ontario L0L 2P0
(705) 429-4936
www.wildcanada.ca

Wildflower Farm
10195 Highway 12 West
Coldwater, Ontario L0G 1T0
1-866-GRO-WILD (476-9453)
www.wildflowerfarm.com

INDEX OF PLANTS
BY BOTANICAL NAMES